Atlantic Journal of Communication

Volume 14, Numbers 1&2 2006

Special Issue on Oppositional Discourse
Special Issue Editor: *Michael Huspek*

INTRODUCTION

Oppositional Discourse: Introductory Statement on its Ideal
and Concrete Forms 1
Michael Huspek

Ideology, Discourse, and Moral Economy: Consulting the People
of North Manchester 7
Colin Barker

Political Analysis Versus Critical Discourse Analysis in the Treatment
of Ideology: Some Implications for the Study of Communication 28
Peter E. Jones and Chik Collins

Analysis of Discourse as "a Form of History Writing":
A Critique of Critical Discourse Analysis and an Illustration
of a Cultural–Historical Alternative 51
Chik Collins and Peter E. Jones

Discourses of Labor Protest 70
Charles Woolfson

On the Philosophical Credentials of the Discourse Society 97
Darryl Gunson

ARTICLE REVIEW BOARD

Mark Aakhus
Rutgers University

Tyrone Adams
University of Louisiana at Lafayette

Jamsheed Akrami
William Paterson University

Janice Anderson
SUNY, New Paltz

Laurie Arliss
Ithaca College

Che Baysinger
Wilkes University

Bruce Berger
University of Alabama

Keith Burkum
Felician College

Margaret Cassidy
Adelphi University

Mary K. Chelton
Queens College

Bryan Crow
Southern Illinois University, Carbondale

Walter Cummins
Fairleigh Dickinson University

Steven Dick
Southern Illinois University

Vincent Filak
Ball State University

JoEllen Fisherkeller
New York University

Donald Fishman
Boston College

John Fortunato
University of Texas at Austin

Katherine Fry
Brooklyn College, CUNY

Joseph Gemin
University of Wisconsin, Oshkosh

Pat J. Gehrke
University of South Carolina

Joan Gorham
West Virginia University

Tracy Gottleib
Seton Hall University

Raymond Gozzi Jr.
Ithaca College

Deborah Greh
St. John's University

Nurit Guttman
Tel Aviv University, Israel

Radha Hegde
New York University

Thomas Heinzen
William Paterson University

Lisa Holderman
Arcadia University

Michael Huspek
California State University, San Marcos

James Hutton
Fairleigh Dickinson University

Roger Johnson
Ramapo College

Thomas Johnson
Southern Illinois University

Barbara Kaye
University of Tennessee

Patricia Keeton
Ramapo College

Peter Kellett
University of North Carolina, Greensboro

Daniel Kolak
William Paterson University

Robert Kubey
Rutgers University

James Kuehl
Fairleigh Dickinson University

Richard Lanigan
Southern Illinois University

Christine Lemesianou
Montclair State University

Barbara Jo Lewis
Brooklyn College of CUNY

Paul Lippert
East Stroudsburg University

Casey Lum
William Paterson University

James Lundy
Xavier University

Odysseus Makridis
Fairleigh Dickinson University

Rosalie Matzkin
Penn State University, Orgontz

Michael Maynard
Temple University

Maureen Minielli
Indiana University/Purdue University

Graham McKinley
Rider University

Simon Moore
Bentley College

Jeffrey Murray
Rochester, NY

John Peterman
William Paterson University

Jeffrey Pierson
Bridgewater College

Mark Popovich
Ball State University

Rudy Pugliese
Rochester Institute of Technology

Lori Ramos
William Paterson University

Brent D. Ruben
Rutgers University

Jack Sargent
Kean University

Jason Scorza
Fairleigh Dickinson University

Ruma Sen
Ramapo College

Jacqueline Sipos
William Paterson University

Linda Steiner
Rutgers University

Daniel Stout
University of South Carolina

Zhenbin Sun
Fairleigh Dickinson University

Paul Thaler
Adelphi University

Geoffrey Weinman
Fairleigh Dickinson University

Carol Wilder
New School University

Andrew Wood
San Jose State University

Paul Younghouse
Fairleigh Dickinson University

Eric Zanot
University of Maryland

Oppositional Discourse: Introductory Statement on its Ideal and Concrete Forms

Michael Huspek
Professor of Communication
California State University, San Marcos

The theme of this special issue presupposes active opposition between agents, conducted by discursive means, and waged within a public setting. In this sense, the term oppositional discourse should not be confused with resistance (a theme of a future special issue in the *Atlantic Journal of Communication*), which often involves latent or suppressed forms of opposition, conducted both discursively and nondiscursively (e.g., in silence), and practiced outside of the parameters of a public setting made unavailable to potential contestants because of disenfranchisement or other modes by which one or more dominant groups have excluded subordinate groups from public participation. With oppositional discourse we are presented with dominant and subordinate groups, to be sure, but they are in public opposition that consists of openly asserted propositions, questions, counters, and other forms of discursive presentation and contestation.

The essays in this volume all point to the critical importance of understanding the manifold ways in which oppositional discourse is conducted. Yet there are significant differences in approach, reflecting a tension that surrounds the very idea of discourse itself. On one side are those such as Darryl Gunson who, following Jurgen Habermas, are content to explore the idealized characteristics of the concept. Just as structuralist linguists have argued that all humans are predisposed to use language in ways that are consistent with what all of us "know" to be syntactic structures or rules, and as speech act theorists have argued that beyond linguistic competence we may have a communicative competence based on "knowledge" of universal rules for uttering speech acts, so there are those who argue that there are universal characteristics of discourse "known" to all speakers. These include, for

---

Correspondence should be addressed to Michael Huspek, College of Arts and Sciences, California State University at San Marcos, San Marcos, CA 92096–0001. E-mail: mhuspek@csusm.edu

example, shared normative background conditions for discursive action such as pure intersubjectivity, hermeneutic sensitivity, reciprocal perspective-taking, all meant to ensure that validity claims can be uttered, questioned, or contested without reservation.

On another side are those who treat discourse as real, concrete expressions produced within larger spheres of human action. Discursive productions, on this view, whether as spoken argument, narrative, dialogue, or as written laws, constitutions, white paper reports, or propaganda treatises, all refer to broader strands of human activity on which they acquire greater or lesser traction in terms of their intelligibility, uptake, and capacity to move agents toward consensus or opposition. Contrary to the idealized view of discourse, therefore, it is not enough to know the constituent elements of agents' discursive knowledge, as the task at hand is to discern what kinds of discourse are being used in this or that specific context, how they are being used, their limits and effects.

Darryl Gunson's essay in this volume is an effort to clarify and expand the idealist approach as it relates to oppositional discourse. Gunson's careful discussion of Habermas's idea of discourse ethics is meant to overcome objections from relativists who are skeptical that such an ethics is indeed part of all agents' discursive "knowledge." A great deal is at stake here. For if Habermas's theory of discourse ethics can be established as that which is already "known" or presupposed by agents, then the theory may be accorded a normative standing and used prescriptively to assess whether discursive practices succeed or fail on moral grounds. Although Gunson argues that Habermas's theory adequately counters the skeptic's objections, his discussion does not direct itself toward concrete instances where dominant and subordinate groups are engaged in advancing claims and counterclaims with the aim of compelling interlocutors or their audiences to arrive at consensus-based conclusions. As such, the following questions go unanswered: If we accept Habermas's theory in its entirety, are there ways by which we can unproblematically apply the normative criteria laid out in the theory? If so, what might they look like? Such questions invite a critical assessment of discourse as a phenomenon that seems more complex than, say, an ungrammatical sentence or a rule-violated speech act. Discourse refers to what may be vast tracts of writing or speech, exchanged between multiple interlocutors in many shifting contexts, and so it is not enough simply to state that one discourse form admits of more or less moral purchase than another. A great deal of additional supportive work is also necessary in establishing the claim to show its applicability in complex contexts. Although Habermas has suggested ways in which a study that combines analytical and normative statements might be possible, neither he nor Gunson has delivered on this count, leaving the idealized theory somewhat hollow and in need of empirical filling in.

That the concept of morality is especially relevant to the study of oppositional discourse is indicated by studies that examine real concrete instances of discursive struggle with the strong insinuation from start to finish that dominant discourses are morally suspect—fraught with internal contradiction, hinged to fundamental untruths, embroidered with deceit, aligned with privileged speakers who have as their strategic goal the suppression or containment of their opponents' voice, and thus producing violent, dehumanizing effects. These same studies go on to suggest that those who oppose dominant discourses are engaged in a form of discursive action that is on some level deserving of moral commendation. Thus we have Colin Barker's excellent discussion of Manchester Health Authority officials' attempts to combine bureaucratic authority and medical expertise within a dominant discourse and how community activists opposed it. In his study, Barker alludes to the moral economy of Manchester's activist citizens, and, drawing on E. P. Thompson's work, notes the activists' embrace of nonmonetary values, traditions, or customs that affirm past practices, and a "conservative" impulse to protect a "pattern of social activity, rights and obligations." The popular discourse that defends the moral economy, he then notes, functions as "a kind of battle cry, or at least a justification for action; and its defense licenses forms of action and speech (for example, physical confrontation with authority, 'imprecations against the rich') which, in the circumstances, might be judged inappropriate." Such characteristics no doubt contributed to Manchester citizens' distrust of the health officials' professional ethic that permitted practices viewed by the citizens as "exploitative" and an "attack on established and valued rights."

Throughout the essay, Barker seems to offer tacit approval of the citizen activists' moral economy and the ways it was realized in discourse: how the people pointed out contradictory truth claims; how they noted the deceit of a doctor using his medical authority to smuggle monetary considerations into the dialogue; how they discerned the officials' unstated biases whereas their own biases were worn openly on their sleeves; how they exposed the officials' "show" at listening as mere pseudo listening. Similarly, Barker notes with some disapproval the Manchester officials' deployment of a capitalist-based professional ethic that condones putting one's own interests first, dismissing community-based rights, and exploiting others for personal–professional gain. It is because the latter prevailed that Barker concludes the following: "The power of argument, it seemed, gave way ultimately to a slightly shamefaced argument of power."

Barker's strong suggestion throughout the essay is that a community-based discourse that is grounded in argument is to be preferred to a range of discursive stratagems routinely deployed in the service of power. But the suggestion remains just that, as Barker does not venture forth with a discussion of what constitutes a genuinely morally imbued discourse. Are there characteristics of community-based discourse that must, by virtue of belonging to the community, be judged as occupying a higher moral plane than a discourse of professional ethics that aims at profit maximization within the context of capitalism? What should those characteristics look like? And what means are available to the analyst to sort them out so as to distinguish a moral discourse of argument from power's strategic uses of argument for monetary gain?

Peter Jones and Chik Collins argue specifically that methods such as Critical Linguistics or Critical Discourse Analysis actually "get in the way of understanding the political and ideological significance of discursive practices and processes" that are evident in oppositional struggle. And as a counter to such methods, both authors argue that "To get at [the] political or ideological significance [of written or verbal acts] we must apply our politically attuned eyes and ears to a concrete analysis of the specific political juncture to which the [discursive act] belongs and contributes in some way ... ." In their first essay, they demonstrate their alternative by considering a truth claim in 2002 by Tony Blair that Iraq possessed and was on the verge of using weapons of mass destruction, and in their second essay they offer rigorous examination of a government-endorsed briefing paper that dealt with Scottish Housing Cooperatives and used deceptive language as an ideological ploy by neo-liberals to dismantle a system of rental housing that for decades had been maintained by local labor councils. The emphasis in both essays is directed not so much toward how the discursive acts as manifested in Blair's text and the government-endorsed briefing paper succeeded in their efforts, or how it is that they escaped immediate detection by those who might have been expected to readily see through the deception of the acts and offer effective opposition. Rather, the authors address how both texts were in fact ideological.

Jones and Collins go on to expose the untruths of both discursive texts, and do so not by means of Critical Discourse Analysis but by "searching out, piecing together, and thinking through a mass of relevant empirical facts." Both authors then go on to suggest that this is what people do in everyday life: "we call on the lawyer and not the discourse analyst to find the catch in the fine print of a contract or on the engineer, rather than the linguist, to find the flaws in a blueprint." On this reasoning, it appears the masses were in need of expert analysts—experienced, well informed, and critically minded participants within the field of ideological struggle or at least "those prepared to immerse themselves seriously and critically in the task of detailed reconstruction of relevant actions and events." Later on in the Jones–Collins' essay, the authors offer clarification as to what distinguishes the expert from the lay person, as the authors state that their analysis "presupposes the requisite theoretical understanding of the relevant phenomena—surplus value, the capital-labor relation, the capitalist state, and, not least, social democracy in Britain—but exactly how the bodies of theory we may draw on relate to newly unfolding events or conjunctures is an open question which requires difficult intellectual labor in the course of which the theories themselves may be revised or modified."

Although Jones and Collins invoke the need for requisite theoretical understanding of the relevant phenomena, at the same time their analyses are relatively silent with respect to theories of discourse, outside the purview of Critical Linguistics or Critical Discourse Analysis, that might inform their specific analyses of how the real truth contents or intentions of discursive acts are recognized or not by their interpreters. Do not some procedures, more so than others, facilitate discursively produced acts of deception? Are not some procedures more conducive to truth-telling or discursively articulated challenges to truth claims than are others? More specifically, why is it that so many lay interpreters of Tony Blair's words or the government-endorsed briefing paper proved unable to have seen through it as have the authors? Were not certain procedural conditions that attended to discourse processes—degree of publicity of the texts' production, openness to challenge, willingness of text producers to discursively engage skeptical interlocutors—lacking that might have instigated greater recognition of the texts' deceptiveness and hence opposition to them? And, perhaps most important, do not such questions beg some theoretical treatment of what discourse processes should look like if opposition is to crystallize and attract potentially sympathetic others?

Charles Woolfson examines the dominant state discourse of "democracy" and "new market economy" in postcommunist Lithuania as a significant means by which the state has rationalized "deterioration in wages and working conditions of labor, and the growth of high levels of unemployment." Woolfson then writes sympathetically of emergent oppositional discourses of labor as depicted in protests, slogans on banners and placards, protest manifestos, and declarations. Among the emergent forms are those of individualized and desperate protest, personalized protests that sometimes involve small quiet pickets of perhaps a dozen standing with placards in dignified order outside MP's homes, and "muted" collectivist discourse of workers who, because of prohibitions against the right to strike, have engaged in public protests in the form of public "walks" during the workers' lunch breaks, "sit-ins" conducted at the end of work shifts, and hunger strikes.

Woolfson points out that the emergent discourses of opposition have not yet gained traction within the larger society and developed into more widespread protests and shows of labor solidarity. And he suggests that among the many reasons for such are continued harassment of workers by authorities, nonsympathetic media coverage, and a welter of antiprotest ideology ranging from symbols of nation to the restrictions of law itself. Against these limits, Woolfson holds up the hope that Lithuanian workers might succeed in bringing about free collective bargaining as one possible avenue of effective discursive contestation. Woolfson seems to assume throughout, therefore, that limits on workers' protests are morally defective and that free collective bargaining is morally commendable. Yet is it not conceivable that some readers with ideological leanings sympathetic to the "new market economy" in postcommunist Eastern Europe might view the limits Woolfson describes as necessary, and perhaps even desirably so? Similarly, might not some readers view workers' right to strike or free collective bargaining as imposing undue strains on postcommunist Lithuania? In the face of this, it would seem incumbent on Woolfson to raise and address questions such as the following: Are there not a minimal set of social expectations regarding the availability of discursive options that override the contrary social interests of those who might have the most to lose by openly free discourse? On what grounds should workers be free to engage in public opposition to state-imposed ideology and practice? And what should the processes allowing such look like if they are to ensure genuinely free expression?

Barker, Jones and Collins, and Woolfson provide superb descriptive analyses of how oppositional discourse either fails or comes up short in the face of power and domination. In Barker's case, the community hospital was shut down; in the case of Collins and Jones, the government-endorsed project to dismantle community housing in Scotland encountered less opposition than might otherwise have been expected; and in the case of Woolfson, Lithuanian workers' nascent protest forms have thus far run up against a high wall of state-sponsored obstruction. In each case, the readers are expected to sympathize with aggrieved oppositional groups. Yet these groups received little sympathy from their opponents and have indeed encountered difficulty in effectively overcoming dominant ideology and practice on the way toward attracting broader based community support. The suggestion here is that perhaps some added burden needs to be shouldered by the analyst—one that goes beyond critical description and argues why it is that oppositional groups have a more compelling moral claim to discursive legitimacy than do the elites they counter—and that beyond the concrete obstacle of being denied sufficient public space to articulate their opposition, there are good reasons for expanding publicity, reasons that have a higher moral purchase than do sectarian social interests.

Ideology, Discourse, and Moral Economy: Consulting the People of North Manchester

Colin Barker
Department of Sociology, Manchester Metropolitan University

"I don't know what you mean by 'glory'," Alice said.
   Humpty Dumpty smiled contemptuously. "Of course you don't—till I tell you. I meant 'there's a nice knock-down argument for you!'"
   "But 'glory' doesn't mean 'a nice knock-down argument'," Alice objected.
   "When I use a word," Humpty Dumpty said, in rather a scornful tone, "it means just what I choose it to mean—neither more nor less."
   "The question is," said Alice, "whether you can make words mean so many different things."
   "The question is," said Humpty Dumpty, "which is to be master—that's all."
(Carroll, 1939, p. 196)

When we seek to understand a word, what matters is not the direct meaning the word gives to objects and emotions — this is the false front of the word; what matters is rather the actual and always self-interested use to which this meaning is put and the way it is expressed by the speaker, a use determined by the speaker's position (profession, social class, etc.) and by the concrete situation. Who speaks and under what conditions he speaks: this is what determines the word's actual meaning. (Bakhtin, 1975/1981, p. 401)

IDEOLOGY AND STRUGGLE

Thinking about oppositional speech and ideas necessarily implicates a number of classic issues in social theory, concerning ideology and discourse. A single article

---

Correspondence should be addressed to Colin Barker, Department of Sociology, Manchester Metropolitan University, Geoffrey Manton Building, Rosamond Street West, Manchester M15 6LL, England. E-mail: c.barker@mmu.ac.uk

cannot aspire to explore all these matters adequately. But we can, at least, search for an approach that avoids some obvious pitfalls.

Theorizing about ideology has two faces. The first looks at how ("dominant") ideologies contribute to stability, with ideology appearing as system, as "second nature," as *habitus* and *hexis* (Bourdieu, 1990). The second, perhaps less familiar, views ideology as a zone of disturbance, of conflict and contest, marked not only by ruling hegemony but equally by creative impulse, innovation, doubt, ambiguity. What makes the second more promising is that, although not doubting the existence of apparent continuities and permanences in thought and speech, it can explore them as "constituted out of flows, processes and relations operating within bounded fields," posing questions about how such processes are constituted and sustained, and about their inner tensions and contradictions (Harvey ,1996, p. 50; see also Abbott, 2001).

Accounts of ideology as a means of social regulation from above, where elites mystify the masses by shaping popular perceptions through discourse and ritual, assume unwarranted coherence within ruling classes and allow no room for meanings and symbols to be contested. Ideologies are rarely homogeneous, but rather, are "usually internally complex, differentiated formations, with conflicts between their various elements that need to be continually negotiated and resolved;" in any case, they exist only in relation to other ideologies, and must negotiate with these, producing an "essential open-endedness" (Eagleton, 1991, p. 45). Scott (1985, 1990) suggested that we look, within hegemonic "public transcripts," for the "loopholes" that provide subordinates with justification for criticism and resistance, even if this achieves no more than covert expression. "Any ruling group, in the course of justifying the principles of social inequality on which it bases its claims to power, makes itself vulnerable to a particular line of criticism" (Scott, 1990, pp. 102–103). "Hegemony" is never complete, for the many-voiced nature of speech always creates some room for alternative meanings to be asserted and explored. And there are motives to search for such alternative standpoints: power breeds humiliation, wealth breeds poverty, exclusion breeds longing. Hence, as Williams (1977, p. 112) remarked, hegemony has "continually to be renewed, recreated, defended, and modified."

Inattention to subordinates' concrete speech and practice appears, multiplied, in those (structuralist and poststructuralist) accounts of ideology as something going on behind people's backs, "interpellating subjects" so that they cannot avoid colluding in their own domination. The ideological appears somehow quite independent of social action and organization, and often far too holistically, as if it were a coherently structured body of ideas imprisoning popular thought and speech.

We can"t consider ideologies without considering their key constituent, language; ideology is "discursive." "The word," declared Vološinov (1929/1986, p. 13), "is the ideological phenomenon par excellence." Ideology is "a process of producing shared meanings of social relations ... it and discourse are inseparably tied" (Steinberg, 1994, p. 507). In this view, discourse is not a "text," as in postmodernism, but is a process of social interaction. It lives, as Bakhtin put it, "only in the dialogic interaction of those who use it" (1984, p. 143). Contrary to the provocative poststructuralist assumption, that "meaning makes subjects and not subjects meaning" (Joyce, 1994, p. 13), it is indeed people who create, and modify, meanings in the course of their interactions. Speakers and listeners are active, purposive "agentic" beings using language to achieve ends. Language, being intersubjective, is inherently dynamic. The meanings it imparts are never fixed by the socially shared signs that compose it, for part of the meaning of human utterances is conveyed by their "evaluative accent" or "tone" (Rochberg-Halton, 1982; Volosinov, 1929/1986). Meaning is constrained and expressed by the context of ongoing dialogue. The meanings of words, indeed, are often contested. As, in the course of social relations, groups and classes of people struggle with each other, they establish shared and "partisan meanings" in language (Steinberg, 1997), contesting the "tenure" of specific terms, indeed "poaching" words from the discourse of other groups to make them their own. This is not to deny that such contests are conducted on uneven ground, that there are dominant ways of saying and meaning, or that categories and frameworks of understanding are often difficult to occupy and invest with our own meanings (Collins, 1999). Yet there is always a potential for subversion within language—by jokes, parody, and all means to actual capture and conversion—and commandeering words for purposes opposed to those whose "property" they might seem. By challenging meanings, those below can begin to develop outlines of alternative conceptions of the world, of their own worth and possibilities, even if often in patchwork form, as emergent oppositional languages for struggle.

The ideological is an inherent aspect of larger ongoing struggles between rulers and ruled for hegemony, involving local battles to invest particular words and phrases with preferred meanings. Rather than pitting one discursive construction against a completely different alternative, challengers engage in more piecemeal processes of questioning particular meanings in given social settings. In so doing, they can draw on "discursive repertoires" (Steinberg, 1999a) that reveal their understandings of wider issues of equity, justice, and order. Often their successes are no more than partial, for challengers often lack other resources (institutional bases, adequate sanctions) to impose and articulate their own understandings.

ARGUMENTS IN TWO PUBLIC MEETINGS

In the light of the aforementioned discussion, this article considers a specific case of oppositional speech, drawn from a study in North Manchester, England, in the mid-1990s of people campaigning to save a local children's hospital from closure. Booth Hall Children's Hospital was a long-established facility, held in considerable esteem in a predominantly working-class area. The threat of closure by the Manchester Health Authority initiated local protest campaigns. These attracted tens of thousands of petition-signatures, organized street stalls, meetings and marches, and a brief sit-in within an unoccupied ward at the hospital. The local town councils in the affected area passed unanimous resolutions opposing the closure, and a readers' poll by a local newspaper recorded a vote of 1,004 to 3 against closure. "Public opinion" could hardly have been more unanimous.

Existing administrative regulations required the Health Authority to engage in "public consultation" about its plans. To meet this requirement, administrators booked several local halls and invited the public to meet them. Transcripts of recordings at two of these meetings, at Moston and Middleton, provide the basis for what follows.

Those attending these "public consultations" were already active campaigners against hospital closure. The meetings were thus predefined as arenas of combat. Although the audiences did not know who would speak for the Health Authority, or what precisely would be said, they were primed to listen carefully for any weak points in the Authority's arguments, and oppose them.

The ways the audiences responded to the Health Authority's arguments depended on what the Authority's spokespeople — mostly paediatricians and health service managers—argued, and how they argued it. Some of their case for closure was listened to in silence, although other parts were sharply questioned, and others again met with noisy interruptions, laughter, and abuse.

The Authority spokespeople argued their case predominantly on "medical" grounds. First, they suggested, the existence of two children's hospitals in Manchester, involving division of their specialist staff over two separate sites, made for medical inefficiency. Second, less children's beds were needed across the area, because of changes in medical technology: the advent of personal nebulizers, for example, meant asthma sufferers no longer need to spend long periods in the hospital. The Health Authority proposed to replace Booth Hall with a new children's ward at the local general hospital, and to expand the range of community-based medical services available to children and their parents in their own homes.

At first, the audiences seemed to have no answer to these arguments, although they were quick to catch apparent contradictions in the Authority's presentation. They had fun with one consultant, who claimed both that his work was interrupted by having to move a few miles from one local children's hospital to another, and that he regularly traveled some 80 miles to another hospital in Barrow-in-Furness. "Barrow!" was a popular heckle during that meeting.

However, such victories were small. Speakers from the floor lacked access to the kind of knowledge with which to undermine the "medical" case. Although, in a poll, most local general practitioners had opposed the hospital's closure, none of these doctors, who might have questioned the official spokespeople's expertise, attended the meeting.

In that sense, the medical arguments became what Bakhtin termed an "authoritative word," not really open to discussion or modification.[1] Except, that is, for one

---

[1]Bakhtin (1975/1981, pp. 341–346) discusses the distinction between "authoritative" and "internally persuasive" words. Elsewhere he uses such terms as "inert" and "sacred" words for the former idea.

question: What would replace the existing hospital facilities? At the first meeting, the Authority offered plans for a new set of community-based services for children. The chief executive explained as follows:

> Chief Executive: Children, by and large, are well. It's a minority of children that are unwell. And a minority of that minority that do have to go to hospital. The technology of health care is changing and we can treat more children in a community setting. Keep them in their home if at all possible in a safe environment.

At first these ideas were not challenged. But then a woman in the audience (a local Labor councilor) rose to say the following, in a speech interrupted by general applause:

> Woman: And now the lady on the end — the consultant, whatever she is, about this er. I get the feeling that we're going to get a "Care in the Community" for children now, which we've got for the old people. Which we all know has not been working for the last twelve months. This is what it comes to me... (*Cries of* Hear hear, *and clapping*) ... So if you can't do it for the pensioners of the country you're certainly not going to do it for the children of the country.

Once that theme had been enunciated, others picked it up:

> Woman: I'd like to say to Dr Ferguson that what you're describing is absolutely wonderful and if you could guarantee that then fine. But we've seen Care in the Community, we've seen the mentally ill and how they're cared in the community. We've seen the geriatric patients and how they're cared for in the community, and we don't trust what you're saying because it doesn't work.
>
> Dr. Ferguson: But it's beginning to happen all the time while you watch. There are more and more children...
>
> Woman: How many have to die ...?
>
> Dr. Ferguson: Nobody's died.
>
> Woman: ... before. People are dying. People are being killed by the mentally ill because they haven't got a hospital bed. Now you're saying that's your dream for the future.

With each new development of this theme, the antagonism grew more confident. The final speaker from the floor at Moston added a significant social generalization:

> Woman: Can I just say that I er although part of me agrees with er Care in the Community I'm also very worried about it and I'm very worried about the pressure that

that puts on working class people. Because to me Care in the Community is a middle class theory and to nurse at home lots of women in working class areas, and in middle class er societies, have to nurse elderly relatives, sick husbands and they have other children and now what we're talking about is bringing other sick children with nurses popping in and out and everybody else in to your home and I just find

Chair: Okay.

Woman: absolutely appalling and

Chair: Care in the Community

Woman: and I'd like to know when are you consult with people like me on this stupid idea of Care in the Community with our children.

Reviewing the evening's proceedings afterward, like sports fans after a game, protestors recalled the speeches on "community care" with especial relish.

STRUGGLING OVER WORDS

The arguments about "community care" in North Manchester involve a struggle over the "tenancy of the sign", that is, over who shall use a term, and how. The word "community," Williams (1988) suggested, is always a "warm" term, which "seems never to be used unfavorably, and never to be given any positive opposing or distinguishing term" (p. 76). In similar vein, Muncie and Wetherell (1995) argued that "community"—along with other terms like "family" and "neighborhood"—forms part of a signification system, or chain of concepts and associations, which includes other key terms like "natural," "harmonious," "organic," "healthy," "warm," "evolving," "personal," and so forth. Governments, they contend, attempted to deploy the term "community" to justify what turned out to be cuts in public welfare spending. The term's connotations, they suggest, can inhibit or confuse opposition: "The argument against community care is rendered more difficult by the reassuring humanistic imagery of neighborliness, close ties, social support and a lifestyle more akin to a mythical image of village life than the urban housing estate" (p. 56). By 1994, however, the North Manchester audience's speeches indicate that "community" could be used—especially linked to that other warm word "care"—as a term of *suspicion*. It had become associated with privatizing and closing public services, in both the mental health and geriatric fields. When the first woman speaker invoked that sense of suspicion, provoking rapid applause from other protestors, she was opening the way to a cascading series of criticisms. The second speaker amplified the opening theme by connecting "community care" with killings by mental patients, whereas the third went on to critique the whole idea of "community care" as a "middle-class" imposition on working-class families. She challenged sentimental accounts of both "community" and "family" by referring to the toil and trouble of managing a household with a sick child.

In the course of the meeting, speakers creatively picked up these variable associations, turning the Authority's own words into weapons against them. As Bakhtin (1975/1981) insisted, words are "multi-accentual:" they do not relate to things in singular ways, but are regularly remade in use within the "elastic environment of other, alien words about the same object, the same theme" (p. 276). The protestors did not challenge the single word alone, but its location within a whole "interpretative repertoire," its practical theorization. Their struggle was not merely linguistic, but over the social practice the word represented and threatened.[2]

The most promising theoretical framework for discussing these interchanges is provided by the "dialogical school" initiated in postrevolutionary Russia by such figures as V. N. Vološinov, M. M. Bakhtin, and P. N. Medvedev, along with Lev Vygotsky. For these thinkers, the study of speech should not be left to linguistics. Human discourse must always be considered in the context of speakers' and auditors' ongoing social relations. Language is an entirely social phenomenon, which must be studied in action, as people use it in social life.

The fundamental unit of study, the "cell form" of dialogue, is not the word, sign or sentence, but the utterance given by a speaker to a listener (or "addressee"), in a definite context. Every utterance involves this person addressing that person, in a particular manner and for a specific purpose. Utterances are pregnant with social life and intentions. We should think of speakers and audiences alike as if on springs, coiled for interaction, actively engaged in mutual communication. Speaking—as the cognate school of rhetorical social psychologists argues—is not distinct from acting, but is itself a form of action, a social practice with its own "action orientation." Most discourse, wrote Eagleton (1991)—borrowing from J. L. Austin—is "performative" rather than "constative," aiming not merely to provide information, models, rules, directions, but to influence the practical and ideological orientation of those who hear it. Speakers' social purposes shape the rhetorical devices and evaluative tones they deploy.

Dialogical theory is distinctive in its attention not only to the producers of discourse but also to their audiences. Far from treating addressees as passive receptors, Bakhtin (1955/1986) insisted on their active and responsive stance; they are beings "full of words," with all their own experiences and "apperceptive background" encoded in inner speech, critically appraising what they hear.[3] Any single utter-

---

[2]There is an account of a not dissimilar battle over the words "negotiate" and "cooperate" during the 1971 work-in at Upper Clyde Shipbuilders in Collins (1996, 1999).

[3]The American pragmatist Charles S Peirce's account of language use has many resonances with the Russian dialogician. He distinguishes between two kinds of "sign"—that provided by the speaker as against the "interpretant" sign of the listener—stressing the difference between these two forms in conversation and life. There is a valuable account of Peirce's views in Rochberg-Halton (1982).

ance is but one event in a chain of dialogical exchanges, itself constructed as an active response to what has been said before. Listeners, attending to other persons' utterances, are already preparing their answers.

Speakers and listeners share a common language with shared meanings, else there could be no communication between them. But within that shared language they impart their own "senses" to words. Individuals "individualize" and "subjectivize" word-meanings, in line with their own social locations, particular experiences, and perspectives.[4] They thus both reproduce and modify, share and contest the significance of language. All manner of politically sensitive terms have this conflict of meaning and sense running through them: think only of such terms as "socialism" and "capitalism," "management" and "workers," "democracy," "freedom," "market," "equality," "racism," and "justice," and so on and on. The class struggle runs through the language, about the language, for control of the language.

The protestors who claimed "tenure" of the word "community" largely succeeded. Summing up at the end of that meeting, the Health Authority chairman acknowledged the following point:

> I think fourthly we're agreed erm on er the importance of developing, I'm not sure we are agreed on this, but I think the support for the delivery of community services if we could get past the skepticism that it's let down the public in other areas like old age and mental illness, there's a lot of skepticism about it
>
> (comments from floor)
>
> but but supported it could be done right.

By the time of the next meeting, a few days later, the Health Authority dropped all mention of its "community medicine" proposals. It was the protestors' opening speaker who offered this theme, now in an offensive vein. Holding up the Authority's document, he declared the following:

> This booklet is riddled with one central concept, and that is Community Care .... That rhetoric, that theme, is actually masking the real central core, the objective is to close Booth Hall.

The Health Authority, once burned by "community care," declined to play with that fire again.

---

[4]The "meaning/sense" distinction is drawn most sharply by A N. Leontyev (1978), a pupil of Vygotsky.

"IT'S ALL ABOUT MONEY"

Active listeners evaluate the status of what is said but also, simultaneously, of the person speaking. Orienting themselves toward others in dialogue, speakers and listeners "place" their interlocutors, forming pictures of who those others are and what they might want (Hall, 1995). In the consultation meetings, such evaluations proved damaging to the Authority's cause, for the protestors questioned not simply the Authority's arguments, but their motives and their trustworthiness.

The audiences granted some legitimacy to medical personnel, so long as they were discussing strictly "medical" matters. However, they strictly de-limited this legitimation. They rapidly challenged the consultants if they strayed from their medical expertise into other matters—and notably into issues concerning money. This happened at both meetings. At the first meeting, a woman pediatrician was heard in silence as she presented the Authority's case for unifying specialist services, until she began to talk about financial advantages. Here the audience became restive. She worsened matters worse for herself by offering an analogy:

> Suppose you had half your family in one house and half your family in another house and you've got to run the rates and the rent and poll-tax and God know what else they sting you for ... .

Here audience interruptions compelled her to halt. A speaker from the floor told her the following:

> Woman: Can I just say to Doctor Phillips, I understand you trying to draw analogies, but the analogy you're doing is basically very much the Mrs. Thatcher patronizing housekeeper's basket ... (*applause*) ... I think we do understand that analogy. It's extremely patronizing to think that we that is the level you have to come to try and explain budgets to the community.

Here, that multi-accented word, "community," performed a new duty. Repopulated with new meanings, it now referred to people hostile to patronizing by doctors. The doctor's "medical" persona was discounted as she was re-identified as moving in the same linguistic universe as an immensely disliked politician, whose "economics" were deeply mistrusted.[5]

---

[5]Hill (1990) has summarized the evidence on "how restricted a purchase Thatcherism [had] on the lower classes and that it was contested by significant numbers even among the service class" (p. 21). Most people, he noted, "still subscribe to the welfare compromise and a 'dependency' culture" (Hill, 1990, p. 21). We might contest his language, but not the content of his argument.

At the second meeting, a male consultant spoke without interruption for several minutes, but then strayed into urging the financial benefits of merging specialist services:

Consultant neurologist: ... for every pound you pull out of your pocket to buy that sort of thing it's a pound less to hire a nurse or a scientist in the laboratory or a ...

(*shouts from floor*): Rubbish

Now why is that rubbish? If you. If you at home are given a fixed budget you have a choice on what to spend it on. The reality ...

(*shouts from floor, the chairman intervenes to restore order, but the doctor has temporarily lost his speaker's authority*)

A pensioner from the floor: It's all about money all the time.

Chair: The whole world's about money, love.

(*shouts from the floor*)

Chair: Dr. Newton may we progress please, if we could progress ...

Later, when Dr Newton referred in positive terms to the "purchaser/provider split" in the Health Service, he was heckled. He ploughed on through interruptions:

Now in the new system everything that happens a bill is raised for it, but the money from the purchasers instead of coming to Pendlebury will go to Hope and the status quo is maintained. So there's no actual change it's just erm a financial arrangement.

(*sarcastic laughter*)

Man from floor: Sack the managers.

The Booth Hall Campaign secretary told him the following, to applause:

I want doctors who are doctors, I don't want doctors who are frigging accountants. I want. I don't want purchasers and providers, I want doctors and nurses in our hospitals running it and I don't appreciate hearing consultants, paediatricians or whatever adopting this terminology which is totally bogus. If the man could concentrate on the job for which I hope, I'm sure he's very good at it, but if he would concentrate on that.

When the doctors raised questions about money, the audience opposed them, and in so doing called their social roles into question. Wandering into the contested sphere of "political economy," they faced audiences who recognized immediately what kinds of language to mistrust and to challenge. What you're actually doing, the audiences charged, is pursuing an alien "monetarist" philosophy, seeking to cut the health services we enjoy—and when you deny it we simply don't believe you.

Audience members repeatedly asserted that, behind their claims, the Authority possessed a covert agenda they dare not assert in public. The Authority's Chief Executive opened the Middleton meeting with the following words:

> Let me make two very clear unequivocal points by way of introduction. The first is that this not about saving money on Children's Services ...
>
> (*sarcastic laughter and comments from floor*)
>
> Man's voice from the floor: Big joke.
>
> (*comments from floor*)
>
> Chief Executive: I I'm sure you'll disagree with me later ... .

And when he repeated the point at the end of his opening address, a woman near the front inquired as follows:

> Do you mind if we laugh again?

and a man in the audience called out:

> Rubbish. Tell the truth.

At the Moston meeting, a pensioner asked the following, rhetorically:

> What is your real reason for wanting to close Booth Hall? What is it? Money to balance the books. (*applause*)

The chairman noted that the question had been asked "almost with venom."

Again and again the same charges flowed freely. Bigger hospitals, said one activist, "mean more money for the bureaucrats who manage them." One floor speaker described the officials on the platform as follows:

> They don't deserve to be on there because they're just money grabbers, put there and paid by the Tory government.

And one woman told them the following:

> Woman at Middleton: You're not willing to put your money where your mouth is and that's why we don't believe a single word that you say. And if the money's gone down from forty million six years ago that it would have cost to provide a hospital down to fifteen or twenty million I bet you any money that you could improve Booth Hall site and provide all those services on that site well for that price. Or has somebody like Eddie Shah already offered you the money for that site? (*applause*)[6]

The theme of "money" kept coming up in different ways. The platform members were accused of attending the meeting only because they were paid, whereas the audience members were there because they cared. The Authority wanted, speakers alleged, to close Booth Hall to sell off the land to private developers. Our scale of values is different, the Authority was told: we pay happily for Booth Hall, but should we be paying for you?[7]

> Man at Middleton: We were clearly told that the Health Trust could not afford two children's hospitals. This town has never decided that it cannot afford to save children's lives. We don't want some sycophants coming in telling us that we have. If it takes more money, then we have to go back to government and say that we want more money. I'll leave you with a question. How much does it cost to employ a nurse and how much does it cost to employ you lot sat on that table coming here to tell us something we don't want to hear? (*applause*)

Running through a whole series of contributions, interruptions, and heckles at the meetings was an effort to "de-credential" the Authority's speakers, by challenging their personal or social character.[8] The Authority's spokespeople were accused of bad faith, of being "minions" of the Tory minister of Health, of changing their story from meeting to meeting, and of attempting to run down the hospital secretly even before the consultation period was over. The officials were called "unelected men in their grey suits and plush offices," who never stayed long in their jobs and thus had no loyalty to the people they were supposed to serve. "You are," one woman told them, "liars and hypocrites." Every remark and gesture by the Health Authority representatives was liable to be taken suspiciously, sometimes with ribald amusement.

---

[6]Again, context is relevant. Eddie Shah had recently attempted to purchase a large piece of public park-land to develop a private golf course, a project defeated in part by another local campaign.

[7]The "money" theme had another side. The audience made its own positive claims to determine the hospital's future. We pay your wages, they told the platform. But also, we have raised large sums of money to buy a scanner for Booth Hall. Over the years, North Manchester clubs, churches, unions, and the like would always give a good hearing to fund-raising efforts for "our children's hospital." "Charity" here meant something different from images of "Lady Bountiful." Embedded in, not imposed on, local working-class life, their own fund-raising founded claims to moral ownership of the hospital.

[8]See Billig (1996) on speakers' "credentialing" work.

The mistrust was amplified by a further theme. Officials had no right to decide the future of the hospital. The protestors knew they had "public opinion" on their side, reminding the platform of how unpopular their plans were, and of how unrepresentative they were of local opinion.

Thus the question arose, what weight did the Health Authority give to local opinion, and to the views of local elected bodies? There was no escape from this. Asked directly what credence he gave to local views, the Health Authority Chairman attempted to divert the question to a competitive theme:

Health Authority Chairman: A lot of credence but I'm not going to advise or my authority will not er in trying to devise the best services for your children and grand-children be just taken over by views that want to defend one hospital. I mean the very remark we had earlier: "Why not move Pendlebury to Booth Hall?" — erm you know, if that was the right solution we'd have a meeting like this round Pendlebury.

But at both meetings he was compelled to acknowledge that he and his colleagues were in the difficult position of saying that they knew better than the people what was in their best interests:

Chair: Again I like to get answers and boil them down. If I can boil that answer down you seem to be saying the hundred percent of public opinion which is against it, apart from the two people you spoke to, are against it because they are ill informed. Is that what you're saying?

Health Authority Chairman: Yes.

(comments from floor)

Chair: Okay, well ... .

Save Booth Hall Campaign Secretary (from the platform): There. There. There's. There's a democrat. There's a democrat.

A MORAL ECONOMY?

As Michael Billig (1995, 1996) noted, thinking and talking involves a complex dialectic of both generalization and singularization. Generalization involves placing an item of experience within a larger category, whereas singularization involves determining which of several potential categories is appropriate, thus introducing a "dilemmatic" quality to discourse and thought. Two features make this more possible. First, the world of "public discourse" or everyday "ideology" is itself a world of argument containing contradictory potentials and oppositions, where "there is no theme without a counter-theme" (Gamson & Modigliani, 1989, p. 6). Second and consequently, people are already "familiar" with idea-sets that they do not themselves necessarily hold all the time, so that their adoption of "new" ideas or their summoning up of "submerged" themes is not a very difficult process, involving merely a shift in rhetorical stance.

Ideological themes persist across time and across populations, their persistence reflecting continuities in social relations and antagonisms. These represent forms of ideological "resource" on which speakers can draw in a variety of situations, as "ways of seeing" (Berger, 1972) which they can assume listeners will recognize and share, providing common "vocabularies of motive" (Mills, 1940). Such persistent themes, however, don't exist in monological or monotonic form, but always in complex dialogical interdiscursive relations with other possible persistent counterthemes (e.g., "class" vs. "nation," "cooperation" vs. "conflict," etc). Further, the importing of such themes into concrete speech always requires attention to the actual setting or situation, including the speech or actions of others.

In a specific interaction like the "consultation meetings" in Manchester, there developed a kind of interpretative contest as to what the meetings were actually about. The Health Authority spokespeople sought to shape the dialogue at the meetings so that, in a sense, it would extend the doctor–patient relationship into the reorganization of the health service itself. They would appear as disinterested professionals, deploying their technical expertise to benefit the population and their children, offering an "education" in the changing realities of medical practice to their client-consumers. The changes we are proposing, they suggested, are in your own best interest, adding that we understand and sympathize with your "feelings." As the Authority chairman summed up the following at the Moston meeting, in a final effort to recredential his side:

> What I hear is that there is a lot of feeling of anger, there's a lot of feeling of distress and worry, and there's a lot of feeling that we're not truthful and there's a lot of feeling that it's finance driven. And I hear those remarks .... We've got to persuade you with more facts and figures that what we're doing is actually to your kids' benefit and is not just to save Mrs Bottomley, or whatever she's called.

But their audiences responded by invoking a different, and antagonistic, "social or evaluative purview" (Bakhtin, 1975/1981, p. 401; Vološinov, 1927/1976, p. 101; Vološinov, 1929/1986, pp. 21, 106) to account for what was going on.[9] One term

---

[9]Vološinov insists that for an item to enter the social purview of a group and "elicit ideological semiotic reaction," it must be associated with the vital socioeconomic prerequisites of the particular group's existence, making contact, even if obliquely, with the bases of the group's material life (1929/1986, p. 22).

that might usefully describe their particular purview is "moral economy." E. P. Thompson developed this term as a means to make sense of the specific "rationality" of 18th century food rioters.[10] It refers to the set of ethical assumptions underpinning resistance to top-down social reorganizations, which were "experienced by the plebs in the form of exploitation, or the expropriation of customary use-rights, or the violent disruption of valued patterns of work and leisure" (Thompson, 1991, p. 9).

A "moral economy" is marked by several characteristics. First, working people identify the cause of some breach in their lives as what Thompson (1991) called "the innovation of capitalist process" (p. 9), where wealthy or powerful figures propose changes at odds with people's needs. The origins of a moral economy are to be found within a capitalist economy.[11] Second, a moral economy affirms a positive counterethic, a vision of the common good entailing nonmonetary values. Third, that vision contains elements of "tradition" or "custom," affirming something already practiced and valued; it is "conservative" in seeking to protect a humanly valuable pattern of social activity, rights, and obligations. Fourth, the enunciation of a moral economy is a kind of battle cry, or at least a justification for action; and its defence licenses forms of action and speech (for example, physical confrontations with authority, "imprecations against the rich") which, in other circumstances, might be adjudged inappropriate.

A moral economy, in this conception, is negotiated, relational, dialogical, constructed, and reconstructed as part of an ongoing interaction between power and powerlessness. Far from being fixed, its precise terms, boundaries, and extent are open to reshaping, challenge, and modification. A moral economy (or almost any other ideological form) should not be viewed as a carefully articulated theoretical system. Rather, it has the character of a loosely coupled and dynamic ensemble (Steinberg, 1999, p. 20) of ideas and evocative symbols, developed in opposition to ruling ideas (which are themselves commonly similar "assemblages" of signs and notions). A moral economy is developed and shared through conversations among its adherents within a local environment of speech or "community of response."[12] Its tenets may be only partially self-conscious, becoming so only when the "tissue of

---

[10]Thompson first used the expression "moral economy" in *The Making of the English Working Class* (1963), developing it in 1971 and further exploring and refining it in 1991.

[11]Moral economy takes on its meaning in "dialectic tension" with "market economy" (Randall & Charlesworth, 2000, p. 2). Randall (1991, p. 255, cited in Steinberg, 1995, p. 80) remarked the following, on the moral economy of trade relations among woollen workers: "The origins of the moral economy therefore have to be found within a capitalist economy, not outside or in opposition to one." This seems slightly mistaken: A moral economy emerges within and against a capitalist economy. Otherwise there is no sense in Thompson's suggestion that moral economy can be seen "constantly regenerating itself as anti-capitalist critique, as a resistance movement" (1991, p. 341).

[12]The term "community of response" was developed in cultural studies by Barker (2000), who identified it as an "essential circulatory medium" for shared evaluations and stances.

customs and usages" it articulates is threatened by "monetary rationalization" (Thompson, 1991, p. 340).[13]

Noting the role of "rumors" — and the rulers' dismissive view of them—in generating 18th-century popular rebellion, Thompson (1991) remarked that the people had direct information sources that could not be easily discounted. In the arguments over Booth Hall, too, "rumors" were significant. Speakers quoted concrete facts: this ward was closed, that section was being moved. In one ward, the window frames were rotten, but new carpet was being laid for offices. Surely, closing a newly refurbished accident and emergency suite was pure wastefulness? Protestors remembered that this child died when no intensive care bed was available. Those parents with a sick child had difficulty getting to the hospital, that child should not have been sent home without an x-ray. The audiences' knowledge might be as piecemeal as many oppositional ideologies, and might often be anecdotal, but it was also concrete. From their social location an overall picture was hard to form, and they were prepared to listen to those with information they lacked and who offered a general perspective. But they listened with suspicion, for that other perspective was "from above," and was always liable to contamination from its contact with others "above," who were known to put their own class interests first.

Given Thompson's (1991, p. 340) own cautions about overextending his concept, is it appropriate to apply the notion of a moral economy to the views of the North Manchester protestors? Cautiously, I think it is. The sense the protestors enunciated was indeed that the Health Authority's proposals represented "innovation of capitalist process." What was going on, they insisted, was exploitation, the expropriation of existing use-rights. For them, the very use of the language of "cost" and "economy" in relation to the Health Service was quite as contentious as the abolition of regulation in the corn trade in the 18th century. The audiences at the meetings were deeply skeptical that the Authority could, in the "monetarist" climate of the time, be proposing anything good; rather, they interpreted the proposals as an attack on established and valued rights. As for children's health care, that was sacred ground.

The audiences expressed a view about what is legitimate and illegitimate in the running of a valued public service, linking this to views of social norms and obligations, and of the proper functions of the several parties in medicine. Doctors and nurses should concern themselves with patients' welfare, and not mix in management politics or start talking managerial jargon. If "management" within the Health Service was permitted any legitimacy, its role was to facilitate the provision of good services for the community, and not to line its members' own pockets or im-

---

[13]In becoming self-conscious, a moral economy may provide materials for some degree of systematization. However, it can be invoked for different sociopolitical purposes. A moral economy may provide underpinnings to a socialist critique of capitalism, for example, but may equally be limited to demands for a capitalist economy modified by a stronger "public service" element (Davies & Flett, 2002).

IDEOLOGY, DISCOURSE, AND MORAL ECONOMY   23

pose alien "market" values. Whatever privileges the rich and powerful might have won in other spheres of social life, health care should be exempt from these. The audiences expressed passionately held views of the common weal, along with a claim that these were indeed the shared notions of the whole people. By contrast, they represented the Authority as embodying an opposed, alien, and vicious agenda.

AUDIENCE ORGANIZATION

The audiences at the Manchester "consultation" meetings revealed a powerful capacity to interrogate the Health Authority's proposals, along with a strongly held set of antagonistic beliefs. They could draw on months and years of everyday talk across North Manchester, and assume a "community of response" for the ideas they expressed. Although each speaker and heckler spoke with his or own individual "accent," speakers were mostly willing to support and encourage each other, and to share and develop common themes in their criticism of the Authority's plans. In the consultation meetings, successful speeches from the floor evoked certain themes—about "community care," about "money," about "democracy," and so on—that other participants could recognize because the currency of those themes in North Manchester made them rapidly familiar. If there was a "moral economy" at work, this is how it was drawn on and recognized. Speakers summoned up an existing stock of ideological resources they could assume others shared, revealing how they fitted this occasion.

The more effective speakers were those who, in a sense, "spoke for the community" through this process of evocation. Their success was marked by responsive markers: they won audience applause, later speakers either referred back with approbation to what they said, or picked up a theme they had opened and developed it further. Those who were especially appreciated were those who found "loopholes" in the Authority's statements through which their own "counterthemes" could be developed.

In the very process of arguing with the Health Authority, the audiences were also evaluating and organizing their own forces. They were not the structureless "crowds" assumed by Le Bon, Freud, and others. They listened, judged, evaluated, discovered—and organized. They rewarded approved speakers with applause, laughter, supportive remarks, waves, smiles, and pats on the back. By such means, they awarded "leadership" status to some speakers. However, they also withdrew or limited that status. At the first meeting, the Campaign Secretary told the Health Authority they were not 'wedded to the bricks and mortar actually on the particular site," and that they welcomed the idea of an expanded community service for children. An Authority manager immediately embraced this remark—for it seemed to suggest they could discount attachment to the physical fabric of Booth Hall Hospital. But the very next speaker from the audience made a point of disagreeing with the Campaign Secretary on the matter of "bricks and mortar," although, as we have seen, other speakers went on to question the "community care" notion. Some speakers from the floor did not attract applause, although they spoke passionately: they failed to enthuse the audience, to make telling points, to enunciate shared themes in convincing ways. Their contributions were awarded no prizes of recognition. By interactively "accrediting" and "discrediting" their own members, the audiences at both meetings gave themselves an emergent shape and direction, thereby recognizing and developing their own ideas.

LIMITS OF DISCOURSE

The North Manchester campaigners could enunciate a powerful "moral economy," they forced the Health Authority to abandon one of its main justificatory claims, and they demonstrated the unpopularity of the hospital closure plan. If anyone could claim "victory" at the consultation meetings, it was the protestors. But that victory had limits. Steinberg's (1994) remarks of ideological conflict that, whereas it can map a terrain of legitimate action and validate contention, it can't organize networks, can't garner resources, and can't take action: "People do that" (p. 515). Realities "beyond discourse" conditioned the passionate speech of the North Manchester protestors. True, they could claim to speak for hundreds of thousands of local people, but only small numbers turned out for a November evening meeting. Angry dissatisfaction at the Authority's proposals was widespread, yet few people were mobilized into more than signing petitions and displaying posters. No campaign demonstration exceeded a few hundred participants. Also, a voice was missing from their own ranks—that of organized hospital workers whose jobs were threatened by the closure. For the most effective of the demonstrations, two hospital porters made their own banner. Carried at the front of a march through Manchester city centre in the summer of 1993, it declared, "Jesus Said 'SUFFER Little Children' SO DO THE TORIES." Such voices were not heard again within the campaigns. No appeals were therefore made to other workplaces for action in solidarity with the hospital workers.

The potential practical sanctions the protestors could bring to bear on the Health Authority were weak. They could speak woundingly, but lacked the capacity to inflict more deadly blows. In interviews, one campaigner described his modest hopes for success: "If we achieve nothing else, at least we will have made them limp." Another reported her own feelings of frustration during the meeting:

> I went to one of those consultation meetings, at Moston Brook, and there people were attacking people on the top table, considerably, very much so ... They were talking very Left. I had the feeling, What could we say? And the thing was, there wasn't anything at that point, because of the way the campaign had gone ... Unless we'd organized people walking out, or storming the platform or doing something

that. I remember discussing it afterwards and feeling dissatisfied with that meeting and the contribution that we'd made. Maybe we should have—but that would have just been a stunt saying, "We're disgusted"—somehow done something along ... In a sense we'd lost the argument by then with the people that mattered, that could turn it round ... . And we did try to build that meeting. I remember doing a lot of going round a lot of people trying to get people to come to that meeting ... . Mostly they didn't come.

The audiences had openly expressed the view that the Authority were knaves or fools, or both. The officials and doctors, more circumspectly, had articulated a view that the people were ill-informed, characterized more by emotional reactions than a rational appreciation of circumstances. Yet, in a sense, the Authority never needed to win the argument, even if they might have preferred doing so. For, as one floor speaker alleged, the meetings involved "pseudoconsultation." The Authority was bound to listen to but not to follow local opinion.[14] It retained the power of decision.

And it would demonstrate this. In January 1995, the Authority held a final meeting in Manchester Town Hall. It was, the chair explained to a sizable crowd, a "private meeting being held in public." At that meeting, in an extraordinary piece of unpopular theater, the members of the Health Authority voted through every point in the original proposals. Their hands went up and down some 20 times, in front of an audience that heckled and insulted them as "puppets." At the end, the Authority members departed rather quickly, leaving a room full of rather stunned and angrily subdued people. The power of argument, it seemed, gave way ultimately to a slightly shamefaced argument of power.

REFERENCES

Abbott, A. (2001). *Time matters: On theory and method.* Chicago: University of Chicago Press.
Bakhtin, M. M. (1981). *The dialogic imagination: Four essays* (M. Holquist, Ed.; C. Emerson & M. Holquist. Trans.). Austin: University of Texas Press. (Original work published 1975)
Bakhtin, M. M. (1984). *Problems of Dostoevsky's Poetics* (C. Emerson, Trans.) Manchester: Manchester University Press. (Original work published 1929)
Bakhtin, M. M. (1986). *Speech genres and other late essays* (C. Emerson & M. Holquist, Eds.; V. W. McGee, Trans.). Austin: University of Texas Press. (Original work published 1955)
Barker, M. (2000). *From Antz to Titanic: Reinventing film analysis.* London: Pluto.
Berger, J. (1972). *Ways of seeing.* Harmondsworth, Middlesex: Penguin.
Billig, M. (1995). Rhetorical psychology, ideological thinking, and imagining nationhood. In H. Johnston & B. Klandermans (Eds.), *Social movements and culture* (pp. 64–81). London: UCL Press.

---

[14]Molotch (1990, cited in Staggenborg, 1993), drawing on studies of ecological protests, suggested that elites have the capacity, after periods of "vulnerability," to recoup their positions. They can organize public meetings as "pseudo-events"—"strictly planned and ceremonious encounters"—where the illusion of popular participation is maintained, while "creeping events" (real events "arranged to occur at an inconspicuously gradual and piecemeal pace") actually determine the outcome.

Billig, M. (1996). *Arguing and thinking: A rhetorical approach to social psychology* (2nd ed.) Cambridge, Cambridge, England: Cambridge University Press.
Bourdieu, P. (1990). *The logic of practice.* (R. Nice, Trans.) Stanford, CN: Stanford University Press. (Original work published 1980)
Carroll, L. (1939). Through the looking glass and what Alice found there. In A. Woolcott (Ed.), *The complete works of Lewis Carroll* (pp. 126–249). London: Nonesuch Press.
Collins, C. (1996). To concede or to contest? Language and class struggle. In C. Barker & P. Kennedy (Eds.), *To make another world: Studies in protest and collective action* (pp. 69–90). Aldershot, Hants: Avebury.
Collins, C. (1999). *Language, ideology and social consciousness: Developing a sociohistorical approach.* Aldershot, XXXX: Ashgate.
Davies, M., & Flett, K. (2002). So bloody much to oppose: The moral economy of privatisation. In C. Barker & M. Tyldesley (Eds.), *Eighth International Conference on Alternative Futures and Popular Protest* (Vol. 1). Manchester: Manchester Metropolitan University.
Eagleton, T. (1991). *Ideology: An introduction.* London: Verso.
Gamson, W. A., & Modigliani, A. (1989). Media discourse and public opinion on nuclear power. *American Journal of Sociology, 95,* 1–38.
Hall, J. K. (1995). (Re)creating our worlds with words: A sociohistorical perspective of face-to-face interaction. *Applied Linguistics, 16,* 206–232.
Harvey, D. (1996). *Justice, nature & the geography of difference.* Oxford, England: Blackwell.
Hill, S. (1990). Britain: The dominant ideology thesis after a decade. In N. Abercrombie, S. Hill, & B. Turner (Eds.), *Dominant ideologies* (pp. 1–37). London: Unwin Hyman.
Joyce, P. (1994). *Democratic subjects: The self and the social in nineteenth century England.* Cambridge, England: Cambridge University Press.
Leontyev, A. N. (1978). *Activity, consciousness, and personality.* Englewood Cliffs, NJ: Prentice Hall.
Medvedev, P. N. (1985). *The formal method in literary scholarship: A critical introduction to sociological poetics* (A. J. Wherle, Trans.). Cambridge, MA: Harvard University Press. (Original work published 1928)
Mills, C. W. (1940). Situated actions and vocabularies of motive. *American Sociological Review, 5,* 904–913.
Molotch, H. (1970, Winter). Oil in Santa Barbara and power in America. *Sociological Inquiry, 40,* 131–144.
Muncie, J., & Wetherell, M. (1995). Family policy and political discourse. In J. Muncie, M. Wetherell, R. Dallos, & A. Cochrane (Eds.), *Understanding the family* (pp. 39–80). London: Sage.
Randall, A. (1991). *Before the Luddites: Custom, community and machinery in the English woollen industry, 1776–1809.* Cambridge, England: Cambridge University Press.
Randall, A., & Charlesworth, A. (2000). The moral economy: Riot, markets and social conflict. In A. Randall & Andrew Charlesworth (Eds.), *Moral economy and popular protest: Crowds, conflict and authority* (pp. 1–32). London: Macmillan.
Rochberg-Halton, E. (1982). Situation, structure, and the context of meaning. *The Sociological Quarterly, 2,* 455–476.
Scott, J. C. (1985). *Weapons of the weak: Everyday forms of peasant resistance.* New Haven, CT: Yale University Press.
Scott, J. C. (1990). *Domination and the arts of resistance. Hidden transcripts.* New Haven, CT: Yale University Press.
Staggenborg, S. (1993). Critical events and the mobilizations of the pro-choice movement. *Research in Political Sociology, 6,* 319–345.
Steinberg, M. W. (1994). The dialogue of struggle: The contest over ideological boundaries in the case of the London silk weavers in the early nineteenth century. *Social Science History, 18,* 505–541.
Steinberg, M. W. (1995). The roar of the crowd: repertoires of discourse and collective action among the Spitalfields silk weavers in nineteenth-century London. In M. Traugott (Ed.), *Repertoires and cycles of collective action* (pp. 57–87). Durham, NC: Duke University Press.

Steinberg, M. W. (1997). 'A way of struggle': Reformations and affirmations of E.P. Thompson's class analysis in the light of postmodern theories of language. *British Journal of Sociology, 48*, 471–492.

Steinberg, M. W. (1999). *Fighting words: Working-Class formation, collective action, and discourse in early nineteenth century England*. Ithaca, NY: Cornell University Press.

Thompson, E. P. (1963). *The making of the English working class*. London: Gollancz.

Thompson, E. P. (1971). The moral economy of the English crowd in the 18th century. *Past and Present, 50*, 76–136.

Thompson, E. P. (1991). *Customs in common*. London: Merlin.

Vološinov, V. N. (1976). Discourse in life and discourse in art (concerning sociological poetics). In N. H. Bruss (Ed.), & I. R. Titunik (Trans.), *Freudianism: A Marxist critique* (pp. 93–116). New York: Academic. (Original work published XXXX)

Vološinov, V. N. (1986). *Marxism and the theory of language* (L. Matejka & I. R. Titunik, Trans.). Cambridge, MA: Harvard University Press. (Original work published 1929)

Vygotsky, L. (1986). *Thought and language* (A. Kozulin, Ed. and Trans.). Cambridge, MA: MIT Press. (Original work published 1934)

Williams, R. (1977). *Marxism and literature*. Oxford, England: Oxford University Press.

Williams, R. (1983). *Keywords*. London: Fontana.

Williams, R. (1988). *Keywords*. London: Fontana Press.

Your Verdict: Keep Open 1,004, Close it 3. (1994, August 11). *Moston Express*, p. 1.

Political Analysis Versus Critical Discourse Analysis in the Treatment of Ideology: Some Implications for the Study of Communication

Peter E. Jones
*Communication Studies,
Sheffield Hallam University, England*

Chik Collins
Politics and Sociology, University of Paisley, Scotland

PRELUDE

Tony Blair, in his Foreword to the document *Iraq's Weapons of Mass Destruction: The Assessment of the British Government*[1] of September 2002, made the following assertions:

> What I believe the assessed intelligence has established beyond doubt is that Saddam has continued to produce chemical and biological weapons, that he continues in his efforts to develop nuclear weapons, and that he has been able to extend the range of his ballistic missile programme ... I am in no doubt that the threat is serious and current, that he has made progress on WMD and that he has to be stopped ... And the document discloses that his military planning allows for some of the WMD to be ready within 45 minutes of an order to use them.

We are interested in how you, the reader, would react to this bit of discourse and so we put to you the following questions, to which we give our own answers later:

- What is your opinion of the claims being made here?
- What considerations would you accept as admissible or relevant in coming to an opinion?

Correspondence should be addressed to Peter E. Jones, Communication Studies, Sheffield Hallam University, City Campus, Howard Street, Sheffield S1 1WB, England. E-mail: p.e.jones@shu.ac.uk
[1]Full text of the document can be found at http://image.guardian.co.uk/sys-files/politics/documents/2002/09/24/dossier.pdf

We begin by asking these questions because they immediately get our critical faculties to work over the text and it is this process of critical interrogation of communicative acts that we are interested in and wish to explore here. It is our contention that an informed and engaged critical response to political communication is not, and does not involve, a "discourse analysis" grounded in what Harris (1996) referred to as "segregational linguistics." We attempt to explain what we think is going on instead and examine the implications of our position for the study of language and communication more generally.

INTRODUCTION

What we present here is the first of a pair of collaborative articles (with Collins & Jones, in press) in which we continue to develop our case against the use made of familiar linguistic methods and techniques in the service of political and ideological analysis by proponents of Critical Discourse Analysis (CDA)—and especially in the work of its leading proponent Norman Fairclough.[1] Each of the articles stands in its own right, but they are also closely complementary. This first article concentrates mainly on the theoretical shortcomings of CDA, tracing these to their roots in the orthodox linguistic conception of language and communication on which CDA is based. The second article is more concerned with the method of discourse critique and uses a particular empirical study of "oppositional discourse" to throw light on the ideological roots and orientation of CDA itself. Although not presented as successive steps in a single argument, the articles together aim to offer a substantial across-the-board challenge—on theoretical, methodological, empirical, and, not least, political grounds—to CDA as well as to its "Critical Linguistics" predecessor (e.g., Fowler & Kress, 1979). We should perhaps add that the authors are in agreement on all main principles although not of exactly the same mind on every issue.[2]

In this first article, we argue that the linguistic methods used by CDA actually get in the way of understanding the political and ideological significance of discursive practices and processes. On the one hand, there is broad agreement between us and the practitioners of CDA that a critical approach to communicative acts involves a grasp of their distinctive contribution to specific social practices. On the other hand, we argue that the CDA brand of "discourse analysis" cannot account for this contribution which does not involve the instantiation or use of an abstract system or systems of verbal forms but rather the creation of unique communicative resources as an integral dimension of the practices themselves. Consequently, we argue, instead, that the contribution that people make or may make, when they communicate, to a particular action, can only be grasped through an exploration of

---

[2]Previous discussions can be found in Jones (2004a) and Collins (1999a, 2000, 2003).
[3]See Jones (2004b) for an outline of some of these issues.

the communicative conduct in its actual place within the unfolding action and only in terms which are specific and proper to that action at the relevant conjuncture. Communicative acts, then, are inseparable in form and meaning from the distinctive composition and dynamic of the relevant field of action into which they are pitched, and as such, demand for their skilled production and interpretation the kind of knowledge and insight that can only be supplied by experienced, well-informed, and critically minded participants in the relevant field, or at least, by those prepared to immerse themselves seriously and critically in the task of detailed reconstruction of the relevant actions and events.

Putting it more simply, a political document, for example, is a matter of politics and a matter for political analysis and judgment. To get at its political or ideological significance we must apply our politically attuned eyes and ears to a concrete analysis of the specific political conjuncture to which the document belongs and contributes in some way; "linguistic" analysis cannot help us with this. More specifically, as we shall try to show, the critical interrogation and interpretation of political discourse involves searching out, piecing together, and thinking through a mass of relevant empirical facts. In other words, to understand and critically respond to communicative practices and products, in whatever domain, we need to know the relevant business inside out. In everyday life, of course, we do not dispute this principle. We call on the lawyer and not the discourse analyst to find the catch in the fine print of a contract, or on the engineer, rather than the linguist, to find the flaws in a blueprint. But it seems as if this principle has been ignored or set aside in CDA in favor of a view in which detailed historical, theoretical, and practical knowledge of the relevant spheres is deemed unnecessary to understanding political and ideological aspects of discourse.

This first article sets out and defends this principle via a critique of the CDA approach to ideology and then goes on to examine its implications for the study of language and communication more generally.

CRITICAL DISCOURSE ANALYSIS

Although there have been a number of attempts to ground a would-be critical social theory on premises and methods borrowed from linguistics,[3] it is Norman Fairclough's version of Critical Discourse Analysis (e.g., 1989, 1992, 1995, 2000, 2001a, 2001b) which, in our view, raises most pointedly the issue of the relevance of linguistics to political and ideological critique. Although the horizons of van Dijk's (1993) CDA, for example, are limited to commentary on what he called "elite discourse," Fairclough (1992) argued that discourse analysis can serve as "a

---

[4]One of the most recent being the application of "Cognitive Linguistics" to ideological matters (cf. Jones, 2001). Others include that of Habermas which is based on the theory of "speech acts" (cf. Gunson & Collins, 1997).

method for studying social change" (p. 1), an argument underpinned by far-reaching claims about the novelty of the processes and trends of social change in "late modernity" (Chouliaraki & Fairclough, 1999). Fairclough (1989) argued that there have been "important shifts in the function of language in social life" whereby discourse has become "perhaps the primary medium of social control and power" (p. 3). Furthermore, Fairclough insisted that "the relationship between discourse and social structures is dialectical" in the sense that "[a]s well as being determined by social structures, discourse has effects on social structures and contributes to the achievement of social continuity or social change" (p. 37). Fairclough has also acknowledged the centrality of class interests and struggle in social change and has paid homage to Marx's contribution (Fairclough & Graham, 2002). For these reasons, Fairclough's CDA is of theoretical interest to us and our renewed attempts to settle accounts with it are perhaps also something of a backhanded compliment to its theoretical sophistication as well as its influence within the field.

A recent article (Jones, 2004a) examined the key historical, political, and economic arguments advanced by Fairclough in support of his claims about the role of discourse. Jones's (2004a) verdict was that the arguments were based either on misconceptions about the workings of particular economic and political processes within capitalist states or on a one-sided or oversimplified general conception of the relations between social being and social consciousness. Jones's conclusion was that "the CDA approach to language involves a mystification of the role of discourse in society. CDA itself, therefore, constitutes an ideological formation" (2004a, p. 119). These issues aside, the justification for applying linguistic procedures to political discourse in the first place can only be that such procedures provide novel and distinctive insights that are essential to our appreciation of the political and ideological workings of the discourse in question. However, Jones argued that Fairclough's (2000) analysis of the discourse of New Labor in fact amounted to little more than a political commentary on labor politics and policies from a rather timid reformist perspective. So-called CDA, in other words, was just a novel way of expressing particular political opinions. On this basis, it would appear that the distinctive contribution of this kind of discourse analysis is not to be found in any genuine discoveries or insights it makes or offers about political communication, but rather, in allowing particular political interpretations and conclusions to be presented as if grounded in established knowledge and procedures in linguistics, and as "a method in social scientific research" (Fairclough, 2001b, p. 121), than as reflecting and expressing particular political predilections and allegiances.[4]

In this article, we build on these arguments in a critical examination of the CDA approach to ideology. However, we certainly cannot do justice here to all the ins-and-outs of this difficult problem. Our focus is on the question of whether a

---

[5]This is essentially the criticism of CDA that has been systematically levelled by Widdowson (e.g., 1998).

consciously critical, politically engaged response to communicative practices and their ideological implications is achievable by discourse analysis in the CDA sense.

CDA AND IDEOLOGY

CDA justifies itself, as did its Critical Linguistics (CL) forerunner (Fowler et al., 1979), by claiming to offer insights into the workings of ideology. The focus on ideology is justified by its importance among the mechanisms of power and social control in "late capitalism" (Chouliaraki & Fairclough, 1999). Thus, for Fairclough (1989), "the exercise of power, in modern society, is increasingly achieved through ideology" (p. 2).

Proponents of CDA, like those of CL, take the further step of claiming that linguistic or discursive structures themselves convey the ideological punch. As Fairclough (1989) put it, the exercise of power is achieved "more particularly through the ideological workings of language ... [which] has become perhaps the primary medium of social control and power" (pp. 2–3). Trew (1979), for example, argued that language structures "are the material existence of ideology" and that his customized version of Transformational Grammar "can be used ... as a means of revealing ideological processes in the production of discourse" (p. 116). Fowler and Kress (1979, p. 198) offered a "checklist of linguistic features which have frequently proved revealing in the kind of critical linguistics we have been doing" and Fairclough (2001b), too, has adopted this "checklist" approach in his version of CDA (p. 126). The checklist is put together using a "framework for linguistic analysis" of lexical and grammatical properties of sentences and texts which "is based ... on systemic functional linguistics" (pp. 130–131). For Fairclough and Chouliaraki (1999, p. 26), ideologies are "discursive constructions" and so issues of "power and ideology" are "best treated in terms of relations between the discourse moments of different practices and different orders of discourse" (Chouliaraki & Fairclough, 1999, p. 63), that is, in terms of relations of identity and similarity in the form and meaning of words, phrases, and other constructions between different texts (so-called "intertextuality;" Chouliaraki & Fairclough, 1999, pp. 118–119). In this spirit, Fairclough (2000) presented his discussion of New Labor politics as "a book about politics and government that approaches them through language, *as language*" (p. 5, our emphasis).

There is no space here for a thorough examination of the view of ideology as the main or most potent force in the production and maintenance of exploitation today, a view that has gained wide currency in academic circles for reasons explored insightfully by Thompson (1978) and Anderson (1976, 1983), among others.[5] To cut a long story short, this view, as Jones (2004a) has argued, is simply false. We say

---

[6]Useful critical discussion of these problems can also be found in, for example, Abercrombie et al. (1980), Thompson (1984, 1990), Eagleton (1991), and Scott (1990).

this, however, not to dismiss the role of ideology in social processes but to emphasize the need to get things in proportion and see them in their proper place. As an aspect of the relatively peaceable exercise of class rule, ideological domination or hegemony generally relies on the possibility of applying force as a last resort (or as a first resort in the case of "rogue" or excluded communities, or far away peoples or states whose lives and opinions do not matter). Furthermore, rule by "consent" is always a partial, precarious, and fragile state of affairs because the maintenance of the very specific social conditions which it presupposes is ultimately outside the control of the ideologists. For that reason, the extent to which ideological means of dominance and control will be effective in deflecting, disarming, or containing resistance and opposition in particular circumstances is always an open question, however much mainstream political debate and media production are dominated by propaganda in favor of those who rule. By the same token, it is unwise to judge the degree of ideological "incorporation" of oppressed and exploited individuals and groups merely on the basis of their everyday compliance, communicational conduct included, with the status quo, because what people say and think in such circumstances is not the best indication of how they will act in changed circumstances, or indeed, is always at one with their actual practice. That is why the consciousness of working people, their degree of radicalization, and their preparedness for political change, can ultimately only be judged in the course of events.

The problems with the "dominant ideology" position are, however, compounded and amplified when ideology is seen in the image of a linguistic system as modeled in a structuralist, "constructivist–structuralist" (Chouliaraki & Fairclough, 1999)[6] or "systemic functional" (Fairclough, 2001) fashion. The problems we have in mind are expressed very clearly in the account by Bennett (2003) of what structuralist linguistics has to offer:

> The "objects" of which language speaks are not "real objects," external to language, but "conceptual objects" located entirely within language. The word "ox," according to Saussure's famous example, signifies not a real ox but the concept of an ox. (pp. 4–5)

Bennett (2003) elaborated as follows:

> This is not to deny that there exists a real world external to the signifying mantle which language casts on it. But it is to maintain that our knowledge or appropriation

---

[7]The term *constructivist–structuralist* combines the sense of linguistic structuralism with that of "constructivism," which means "the assumption that language in interaction is constitutive of the social world and of the self" (Chouliaraki & Fariclough, 1999, p. 48). The authors claim that their view of discourse "as a moment in social practices and as a form of social production ('joint action') in practices entails a constructivist focus on social life as produced in discourse, as well as a structuralist focus on the semiotic (including linguistic) and non-semiotic structures, which are both conditions of possibility of discourse and products of social (including discursive) production" (Chouliaraki & Fairclough, 1999, p. 48).

of that world is always mediated through and influenced by the organizing structure which language inevitably places between it and ourselves. (p. 5)

From this we see that the reward we get for adopting this linguistic view of meaning is the opportunity to surrender our faculties for thought and communication to an "organizing structure" placed as an opaque barrier between us and the world by language. Bennett (2003) never asks how or why language gets to do this, or how this organizing system might help or hinder us in our actual practical dealings with the world, a world which includes the real ox as well as our relations with it. In any case, the premises of this linguistic approach make the question irrelevant or unanswerable; in life, our immediate connections are not with the world but with language: "reality is always discursively mediated — *we have no access to reality except through discourses*" (Chouliaraki & Fairclough, 1999, p. 136, our emphasis).[7] Thus, whatever our practical dealings and experiences may seem to tell us, the language system is responsible for the way we talk about and conceptualize things. If actual communicative acts are always only expressions of, uses of, or instances of elements within the preexisting abstract system, then that makes it impossible for communicative or cognitive actions to go beyond the semiotic, and therefore, ideological limits of the "organizing structure" already in place.

Now, the failings of Saussurean linguistic structuralism have long been known. But these failings are not confined to the idea (obviously false) that all members of the community use the same semiotic system, and consequently, cannot be addressed by allowing "organizing structures"— whether we call them "languages," "codes," "lects," "genres," or "discourse types"—to proliferate along socioeconomic,cultural, or occupational lines, because this proliferation merely reproduces the inherent problems of "abstract objectivism" (as Vološinov, 1973, referred to this trend) in ever decreasing circles.

In our view, the main problem with the whole approach is a matter of the fatal damage visited on rational thinking and action when the connections between ideas and life experience are broken, when the processes of critical thinking and intellectual engagement with real life problems are replaced by the play of words and word meanings within a verbal system abstracted from communicative practice. Hereon it becomes impossible—without being accused of being a hopeless dupe of empiricist ideology—to talk any more about understanding or having an insight into something, or getting to the bottom of things, or, heaven forbid, getting to the truth of the matter.

Accordingly, those who are prepared to view the ideological realm in these linguistic terms have to disconnect ideology from questions of truth and falsity. As

---

[8]The authors add that "the comparative strengths and limitations of different discourses are constantly being judged in the course of practice" (1999, p. 136), but how this could be accounted for in "structuralist–constructivist" terms is not explained, and in practice, CDA avoids examination of the empirical links between discourse and social events.

Fairclough (1995) rightly conceded, "discourse analysis cannot *per se* judge the truth or well-groundedness of a proposition" (p. 18), although it can, apparently, detect ideology provided that we adopt what Fairclough (1995) called the "pejorative view" (p. 18) of it which he explained as follows:

> In claiming that a discursive event works ideologically, one is not in the first instance claiming that it is false, or claiming a privileged position from which judgements of truth or falsity can be made. One is claiming that it contributes to the reproduction of relations of power. (p. 18)

But this sidestep only appears to get around the problem because it begs the question of how we can tell if a discursive event "contributes to the reproduction of relations of power.". This, we would argue, is the fatal flaw at the heart of CDA. We submit that it is actually impossible to judge the ideological flavor or implications of communicative acts independently of a consideration of the empirical facts of the relevant matter. And this for the simple reason that relations of power, although certainly having to do with attitudes of compliance or resistance as well as beliefs and moral values, are not figments of the imagination or figures of speech but real, factual relations between actual people which rest on and are inextricably entangled with such social realities as the ownership of property, wealth, rate, and intensity of exploitation, rights and privileges under the law, institutional authority, political organization, and so on. How particular communicative practices may impact on or influence such practical social realities is itself, therefore, a matter for factual investigation of the relevant chains of action within which these communicative practices have their place and to which they are connected.

Let us attempt to justify our position by returning to the questions we posed to the reader about the Blair extract:

- What is your opinion of these claims?
- What considerations would you accept as admissible or relevant in coming to an opinion?

For our own part, we would start by addressing the second question. Our first consideration might be the veracity of the claims. In the case of this particular document, the claims made are substantially false. It is not just that they turned out to be false when events subsequent to the United States–United Kingdom invasion and occupation of Iraq conclusively demonstrated the complete absence of "WMD," or weapons of mass destruction, to even the most fervent believers, but that informed observers knew at the time that the claims were false or grossly exaggerated; the political and military establishment knew that there was no "serious and current" threat. We would also note that the credibility of this document, and of Blair and his case for war on Iraq, suffered a serious blow with the subsequent publication of what quickly became known as the "dodgy dossier," namely a document with the gloriously understated title *Iraq—Its Infrastructure of Concealment, Deception and Intimidation*.[9] Channel 4 News immediately discovered that "large chunks" of the dossier "had been lifted word for word" from a PhD thesis by Ibrahim al-Marashi but without acknowledging this source.[10] Close textual comparison of the dossier with the plagiarized thesis shows that certain passages had been deliberately altered to beef up the case for war. For example, the original wording, "aiding opposition groups in hostile regimes," turned into "supporting terrorist organisations in hostile regimes." Once this plagiaristic tampering had been exposed, close examination of the actual claims made in the dossier became rather pointless because it was clear that its authors simply did not care whether the material was factually accurate.

A second consideration might be the immediate political context into which the document was pitched. Of particular relevance would be the mood within the general public, some sections of the media and a growing band of Labor MPs, of increasing disquiet about, and outright opposition to, the prospect of an invasion of Iraq. Indeed, the "dodgy dossier" was released on the day of a crucial parliamentary debate on the war, giving no time to skeptical Labor MPs to check it through before the debate.

Furthermore, all these considerations would have to be reevaluated in the broader context of the Iraq war itself—the reasons for the war, the conduct of the war and its aftermath—and in the context of a thorough investigation of what the whole episode has to tell us about the political landscape in Britain in general and about the evolution of the Labour Party and the future of labour movement politics in particular.

With these issues in mind, then, our own opinion of the document is that it was a piece of crude, shoddy, and mendacious propaganda whose immediate aim was to influence—through the party apparatus and the media—the crucial debates and votes in parliament to stave off a major political catastrophe over the war and to continue to deliver the necessary political and constitutional authority to the (long) planned imperialist war of conquest of Iraq. The hysterical clamor about "WMD" provided a pretext but not the reason for the war. The document itself, the fruit of an unprecedented level of political collaboration between Blair's ruling circle and the secret service bosses, was a novel indication of the further degeneration of British social democracy. It demonstrated the complete political putrefaction of the higher echelons of the Labor Party, and as such, should give a clear signal to the labor movement in Britain (and the world)— if indeed it is still needed—that "New Labor" is not their ally in the pursuit of social advancement but their enemy and that the process of political renewal must be pursued in earnest.

---

[9]The dossier can be accessed at http://www.number_10.gov.uk/output/page1470.asp

[10]The references which follow and fuller discussion can be found at http://www.channel4.com/news/2003/02/week_1-07_dossier.html and http://www.channel4.com/news/2003/02/week_1-06_dossier.html

Now, this is, certainly, an analysis of the document, and one in which we focus our attention very closely on the language, but it is not "discourse analysis" in the usual linguistic sense. When we ask ourselves the kind of questions that we posed to the reader earlier—and these are, by the way, the kind of questions that people usually ask themselves about what politicians say—we immediately adopt an attitude toward the language of the text which is at odds with the attitude required to do CDA. In asking and trying to answer these questions, we engage in a process of inquiry which does not work at all in terms of the constructs of orthodox linguistic theory. We are not trying to identify, classify, and trace the words and phrases of the document in terms of their lexical, grammatical, or generic relations to other words and phrases in the same or other documents; constructs of this kind are simply not the stuff of critical interrogation and evaluation. And this is because, when we are reading the words of this document, we are engaging with its author over some matter, we are evaluating and responding to the author's position both with regard to the relevant facts of the matter and toward us as participants in the action. And this process of engaged critical inquiry and response with respect to a particular matter, a process basic to all communication, is something that the linguistic procedures on which discourse analysis rests have signally failed to deal with. Our position, then, is that the political significance and ideological orientation of the document in political terms cannot be established by looking for "relations between the discourse moments of different practices and different orders of discourse" (Chouliaraki & Fairclough, 1999, p. 63), but is something that emerges as we work out how the document is contributing to political events at a particular conjuncture, and, in so doing, penetrate ever more deeply to the heart of the relevant problem.[8] Without reconstructing this whole field of political practice in which the document is placed, we have no chance of a realistic and accurate political and ideological evaluation of it. The ability to make such an evaluation, therefore, depends on what and how much we know and understand about the factual events and circumstances making up particular political conjunctures.

At the same time, such an analysis presupposes the requisite theoretical understanding of the relevant phenomena—surplus value, the capital-labor relation, the capitalist state, and, not least, social democracy in Britain—but exactly how the bodies of theory we may draw on relate to newly unfolding events or conjunctures is an open question which requires difficult intellectual labor in the course of which the theories themselves may be revised or modified.[9] In sum, our interpretation of

---

[11]Ilyenkov (1997) sharply distinguished between "categories"—forms of critical thinking necessary to the cognition of the different spheres of being—from verbal forms and meanings which, in contrast with categories, express superficial commonalities between different phenomena (p. 64).

[12]Ilyenkov (1982) said the following: "It goes without saying that the assimilation of the results of previous theoretical development is not a matter of simply inheriting ready-made formulas but rather a complex process of their critical reinterpretation with reference to their correspondence to facts, life, practice. A new theory, however revolutionary it might be in its content and significance, is always born in the course of critical reassessment of previous theoretical development" (p. 159).

the document is political; it is the result of informed political analysis and it stands or falls by the cogency and coherence (or otherwise) of its overall interpretation of the role and contribution of this particular piece of communication within the political processes to which it belongs.

Consequently, when it comes to trying to interpret a novel piece of communication in the political sphere, there is no guarantee either that we will have all the relevant facts at our disposal, or, even if do, that we will know straightaway what to make of it, and still less, how to respond. Generally speaking, acts of communication do not nail their political or ideological colors to the mast, as we know from the history of debates, splits, and conflicts within 20th-century revolutionary movements, or indeed, from the history of the British Labor Party. Even the examples of Blair's WMD assessment or the "dodgy dossier" show in a rather straightforward way that a concrete analysis of a political communication involves preliminary investigation and detective work to establish what the relevant facts are in the first place.[10]

Because ideology, then, is in fact a dimension or aspect of practice, it cannot be apprehended, identified, evaluated, or responded to as a communicative phenomenon other than through an informed critical interrogation of that practice as a whole in its relevant empirical circumstances and conditions, its factual implications and consequences. Our general conclusion, then, is that the premise of CDA, namely that one can identify ideology in discourse independently of discovery and consideration of the facts of the matter (and, therefore, of the veracity of claims and proposals), is false; the "pejorative view" of ideology is simply incoherent.

Let us illustrate the point with an example of the CDA approach in action.

CDA AND IDEOLOGY IN "REPRESENTATIONS OF GLOBAL ECONOMY"

In Fairclough's (2001b) discussion of a text attributed to Tony Blair in which "dominant," that is, neo-liberal, "representations of change in the 'global economy'" (p. 127) are being presented, Fairclough focused on "one social problem manifested in the text," which is as follows:

> ... feasible alternative ways of organizing international economic relations which might not have the detrimental effects of the current way (for instance, in increasing the gap between rich and poor within and between states) are excluded from the political agenda by these representations. (p. 129)

Fairclough (2001b) is interested in "linguistic features of the text in its representation of economic change" on the grounds that "[d]ominant representations of 'the

---

[13]We should add that the transparent lies and fabrications of the dismal Blair dossier are not even worthy of the epithet "ideological," although there are obviously ideological issues at stake in the continuing influence of the Labor Party on the British labor movement.

new global order' have certain predictable linguistic characteristics"(p. 131). One such is that "processes in the new economy are represented without responsible social agents" (p. 131). His point is that if global economic change just "happens," rather than being brought about as a result of particular decisions and actions, then there is nothing that can be done about it: there are no alternatives and resistance is futile. This is the ideological significance that Fairclough claims can be carried by particular linguistic features and which he claims to find in passages like the following: "The modern world is swept by change. New technologies emerge constantly; new markets are opening up. There are new competitors but also great new opportunities" (p. 131).

Fairclough (2001b) commented as follows:

> Agents of material processes are abstract or inanimate. In the first paragraph... "change" is the agent in the first (passive) sentence, and "new technologies" and "new markets" are agents in the second — agents, notice, of intransitive processes ("emerge", "open up") which represent change as happenings, processes without agents. The third sentence is existential — "new competitors" and "new opportunities" are merely claimed to exist, not located within processes of change. (p. 131)

The procedure of CDA, then, amounts to making claims about correspondences between aspects of sentence structure (described using Hallidayan systemic functional grammar) and the alleged ideological orientation of the relevant text. The whole procedure, in other words, is based on the premise that we can draw reliable conclusions about how particular events or processes are conceptualized from a linguistic description of the sentence.

But this premise is decidedly fragile, to say the least. For one thing, it simply does not follow that Blair, whatever else he may be guilty of, is representing "agents of material processes" as "abstract or inanimate" by writing a sentence like "the modern world is swept by change." And it is not necessarily the case that "new competitors" in the second sentence are "merely claimed to exist, not located within processes of change." Suppose someone says, "the entrance to the stadium was blocked by traffic." Are they representing traffic as a phenomenon without an origin or source in the driving activities of particular people? Or suppose somebody suddenly says, "there is a goat in the garden." Are they claiming that the goat "merely exists" and has not trotted in from anywhere? And what if Blair had followed the aforementioned pair of sentences with a further sentence that actually spelled out who was responsible for the changes in question, such as the following: "All these changes are the fruits of the drive, enterprise and determination of millions of people around the world"?

We are not suggesting that Fairclough is wrong in attributing neo-liberal ideology to Blair or that he is necessarily wrong about his interpretation of these sentences. But we are suggesting that his interpretation is informed rather more by what he knows about Blair's politics than by "grammar." The difficulty that Fairclough has got himself into with this kind of "analysis" is only too clear, in fact, from his own writing. Shown later, for example, are three passages from

Chouliaraki and Fairclough (1999, p. 3), showing how the authors themselves "represent" the social changes of "late modernity:"

(a) The past two decades or so have been a period of profound economic and social transformation on a global scale. Economically, there has been a relative shift from "Fordist" mass production and consumption of goods to "flexible accumulation."

(b) Advances in information technology, mainly communications media, underlie both economic and cultural transformations, opening up new forms of experience and knowledge and new possibilities of relationships with faraway others via television or the internet.

(c) These social changes create new possibilities and opportunities for many people.

The reader will note that the sentences display the "predictable linguistic characteristics" of neo-liberal ideology. In (a), economic and social changes are presented as "happenings, processes without agents." In (b), the "advances in information technology" referred to are "agent-less" and these agent-less processes are themselves the "agent" of "opening up." In (c), it is the impersonal and agent-less "social changes" which are the "agent" responsible for "creating" possibilities and opportunities.

The most charitable interpretation of this episode is that CDA's "checklists of linguistic features which tend to be particularly worth attending to in critical analysis" and which are offered to those "who are not specialists in linguistics" (Fairclough, 2001b, p. 126), are a most unreliable tool for ideological critique. But we are inclined to the more general conclusion that the formal constructs of grammatical description are altogether unsuitable vehicles for the difficult intellectual labor of meaningful political critique. As is apparent in our second article in connection with "socialist housing policy," what appear, from the point of view of linguistic analysis, to be the same or similar words or phrases in different texts, or even in the same text, may not be the same at all from the point of view of the informed reader. The process of understanding what the words are and what meaning they have involves making a decision about a particular bit of communicative behavior on someone's part.[11] And, as we must do for any bit of behavior, we interpret it in the light of what we know or can find out about all the relevant facts and circumstances, including, of course, what has been said and done before on that subject by this person or others.

How, then, we might interpret passages like "the modern world is swept by change" depends on a whole host of factors including how we understand what else is being said and by whom and for what purpose in what context, given what we

---

[14]Harris (1981, p. 193) argued that the "resolution of semantic uncertainties" involves "decision rather than discovery; and it is indefinitely revisable."

know about the politics of its author, the circumstances surrounding the text, and, not least, our own opinion on the relevant facts. Whether we take the passage as an expository move to be followed by an account of the mechanisms of change, as a wistful evocation of the fragility of communal bonds, as a celebration of the impersonal march of historical inevitability, or simply as a piece of clichéd, semantically wishy-washy New Labor-speak, is something that grammatical description cannot decide for us. Moreover, the fact that linguistic methods even appear relevant to the identification of ideology is due to the confusion which the Hallidayan systemic functional approach in linguistics introduces by presenting notions like "agency" as abstract grammatical categories in the first place (see Jones, 2006). Of course, there is nothing stopping people from making political judgments according to grammatical criteria if they so wish. If they see neo-liberal ideology every time they come across a sentence dealing with social change that has an "abstract or inanimate agent," that is up to them. But that does not mean that they are in possession of a method of "discourse analysis" capable of supplying unique political and ideological insights; it simply means that they are the owners of a very bad method of arriving at political judgments.

But it is also a method which has serious implications for the theorizing of the social process as a whole. The tendency in CDA to simply conflate the processes of thinking with the properties of verbal forms and meanings as identified by orthodox linguistic description, and to equate the critical interrogation of communicative acts with a linguistically based "discourse analysis," distorts the real processes of social and political action. In rendering down the living properties of communicative practices into the stable and repeatable forms and figures detectable on the linguistic radar, it introduces a "fictional stasis" (Thompson, 1978, p. 262) into the dialectically developing system of transitions between thinking, communication, and action. And because, as a purely linguistic methodology, it cannot provide a concrete picture of the actual role of communication in social changes, it must, then, posit an imaginary picture in which the social changes taking place today are "constituted to a significant extent by changes in language practices" (Fairclough, 1992, p. 6; see Jones, 2004a, for detailed discussion). A case in point is Fairclough's (2001b) verdict on the ideological function of neo-liberal representations of change in the "global economy." Fairclough's diagnosis of the "social problem manifested in the text" by Blair is that "alternative ways of organizing international economic relations *are excluded from the political agenda by these representations*" (p. 129, our emphasis). From our point of view, however, all the excluding and marginalizing, within mainstream politics and media, not just of forthright anticapitalist critique and action but even sustained and honest factual examination of political events and their history, is being done not by "these representations" but by people; it is a moral and political issue to do with such things as media ownership, the political allegiances and the editorial and management practices of those responsible for media coverage, and the corruption and servile attitudes of most of our democratically elected representatives.

OUR OBJECTIONS TO CDA

The arguments we have presented earlier lead us to the simple conclusion that there is no such thing as CDA because discourse in the linguistic, and therefore, CDA sense, does not exist. Although there can be no objection to using such general notions as "communication," "discourse," "language," or "genre" to refer to and talk about particular communicative phenomena, we reject the CDA understanding and treatment of these phenomena. Our position, in contrast with the practice of CDA, is that the identification of the communicational processes and strategies relevant to particular engagements, the understanding and interpretation of what the relevant or significant communicational forms, meanings, and patterns are in a particular situation or event is something that emerges in the course of detailed empirical investigation of the relevant event in all its complexity. There is simply no method or procedure of discourse analysis to be applied short of this process of deciding what words mean in the course of interpretatively reconstructing an entire action or event to which the words contribute. Within the event itself there is no level or dimension of "discourse" as a self-contained, stable, and iterable system of forms and meanings.

From that point of view, lay parlance is more accurate than the terminology of discourse analysis. In everyday life we do not write, speak, see, or hear "discourse." Rather, we engage with and react to a particular political speech, and to the proposals and arguments made in that speech, a bus timetable, a memo from our superiors, an advertising campaign, an unsightly piece of graffiti, a racist comment, a proposed change to our contract of employment, a confidential report, a theoretical account of communication processes, a set of instructions for using a DVD player, a statistical table, a bit of friendly banter, and so on. Communicative practices and their products are identified and handled according to their factual linkage or integration (Harris, 1996) within particular types of ongoing activity. This does not mean that when we come to interpret these practices and products we do so without any expectations or preconceptions at all to do with what might be communicated or how. It is just that our judgements about what is being said and meant in context, and in particular, our decisions about what to count as "the same thing" in different communicative encounters, are not made in accordance with orthodox linguistic methodology, in which the "tokens" of particular communicative acts are assigned to "types" in the "system" or "code" (cf. Hutton, 1990), but on the basis of what we take to be actually going on in the situation and what role the communicative conduct of those we are engaging with might be playing.[12] Vološinov (1973) put this so well:

> The basic task of understanding does not at all amount to recognizing the linguistic form used by the speaker as the familiar, "that very same," form ... No, the task of un-

---

[15]"The claim is not that speakers cannot produce or recognise instantiations of the same expressions on different occasions, but rather that this ability does not yield a criterion of demarcation between the linguistic and the non-linguistic, nor imply that whatever we say is decontextualisable" (Harris, 1981, p. 155).

derstanding does not basically amount to recognizing the form used, but rather to understanding it in a particular, concrete context, to understanding its meaning in a particular utterance, i.e., it amounts to understanding its novelty and not to recognizing its identity. (p. 68)

The lexicographer, the linguist, the stylistician, or language teacher have terms to describe functionally different "styles," "registers," "genres," "speech genres," and so on, and these classificatory notions have their practical and descriptive value.[13] But the tasks and problems which face communicators in everyday life have a logic to them which subverts any systematizing tendencies which might be implied by an overly formalistic application of such descriptive classifications. Although it does not take much communicative gumption to tell the difference between a legal contract and the instruction manual for a DVD player, whether we should sign up to the contract or how we get the DVD player to do what it says in the manual are communicative tasks of a quite different order to do with the practical integration of particular communicative practices into our lives and ongoing activity, tasks which require us to relate to and evaluate the texts from this practical point of view.

Everyday communicative activity, then, involves exactly the kinds of thing that linguists usually regard as the business of other professionals or disciplines, such as telling the difference between a fair and an unfair legal contract, between a clear and a completely hopeless set of instructions, between a true statement and a false one, between a profound and a simplistic argument, between a viable plan and an unrealistic one, a beautiful or banal account, an inspiring or boring appeal, a betrayal and a loyal commitment to the cause, a reliable or unreliable bus timetable, and, as we see in our second article, between a socialist strategy for public housing and a reactionary one. Even such a basic, but communicationally essential, fact as whether a bus timetable is current or out of date would not usually, as we know, be considered a linguistic or discursive fact, because it involves the practices of establishing and constantly reestablishing a factual link between the document and the world. Harris (1981) put it as follows:

Even the use of ordinary grading words, like *heavy, good, unusual*, typically involves a simultaneous assessment of facts and terminological appropriateness, correlated in such a way that when doubts arise it often makes little sense to ask whether they are factual doubts or linguistic doubts. They may in one sense be a mixture of both, but not necessarily a mixture that could even in principle be sorted out into two separate components. (pp. 180–181)

This is not to deny that the drafting and interpreting of the terms and conditions of a legal contract or treaty, for example, require special knowledge and expertise,

---

[16]See Collins (1999a, 1999b) for a use of the Bakhtinian notion of "speech genre" in the analysis of communicative acts at particular political conjunctures.

and the more the better, in handling legal discourse, in understanding legal terms and concepts and the system of law to which these belong. But it is to emphasize that such communicative expertise in the handling of the language is acquired and exercised only through a simultaneous apprehension of the whole legal system and framework, in theoretical and institutional terms, along with the factual basis on which legal judgments are made, to which legal distinctions relate, and the factual implications of such judgments for particular cases.[14] As the recent storm over the designation of individuals captured during the U.S. invasion of Afghanistan as "enemy combatants" by the U.S. government shows, the application of the law and the appropriateness or otherwise of legal terms is a matter not only of interpretation and decision in relation to the relevant factual details but also, of course, political expediency.

The process in which we come to such judgments and decisions about the meaning, value, and implications of communicative phenomena on the basis of the situated links between communicative and other practices is not something extraneous to language and communication but is the very heart and soul, the be-all and end-all of communicative behavior. This process, when examined carefully, teaches us that when we approach particular communicative acts, we should reject any assumptions, based on the abstract procedures of linguistic analysis, about what the communicationally significant properties of such acts will be. All the myriad practices of actual, historical individuals present circumstantially unique meaning-making activities which are adapted and integrated into the overall course of these practices. How communication takes place in these circumstances, what is being communicated and what the relation is between the communication processes taking place within different practices and different circumstances are all, then, open questions to be decided by informed, concrete examination and analysis of the relevant practices and circumstances themselves.[15]

COMMUNICATIONAL IMPLICATIONS: "INTEGRATION" OR "SEGREGATION?"

We hope it is clear that our objection to CDA is not an objection to the study of language, or, more to the point, to the close study and analysis of discourse. On the contrary, we accept that the study of communicational processes and practices is,

---

[17]Compare Harris (1981, pp. 187–193) on legal decisions.

[18]Compare Marx on the term *Caeserism:* "I hope that my work will contribute toward eliminating the school-taught phrase now current ... of so-called Caeserism. In this superficial historical analogy the main point is forgotten, namely that in ancient Rome the class struggle took place only within a privileged minority, between the free rich and the free poor, while the great productive mass of the population, the slaves, formed the purely passive pedestal for these combatants" (Marx & Engels, 1969, p. 395).

and always has been, an integral and necessary part of any attempt to understand and critically respond to what is going on in the world. Communicative practices can be as decisive in their contribution to the success or failure of a project, and, by the same token, as objectionable on ethical or political grounds as any other aspect of conduct.

Our objection, rather, is an objection to the turn to language and discourse on which CDA is founded; it is an objection to the turn of a certain school of thought in contemporary linguistics for weapons of political and social critique. It is also, most emphatically, an objection to what this procedure entails, namely an effort to take the communicative dimensions of the living processes of social action, conflict, and change and reduce them down to the meager and abstract fodder of linguistic analysis.

To be more exact, we have in our sights those linguistic approaches which Harris (1996) called "segregational." The essence of segregationalism lies in its initial assumption that a clear, generally valid line of demarcation can be drawn between linguistic and nonlinguistic phenomena and in the consequent attempt to identify and systematize a realm of properly and purely linguistic structures and meanings independently of the actual situated practices of communicative interchange in their empirical complexity. The result is a conception of linguistic communication as a process which presupposes and expresses an already established and more or less self-contained, more or less stable, intersubjectively shared and recognizable "code" or system of form-meaning correlations (or "signs"), a conception which Harris (1981) dubbed the "language myth."

As Harris (1980) argued, the segregational conception is based not so much on a careful exploration of situated communicative practices as on the theoretical glorification and elaboration of a preconception about communication and one which already embodies a certain view of social relations and processes. Saussure's linguistic theory, for example, in "its quasi-mystic appeal to the absolute sovereignty of the community, its deliberate subordination of the linguistic role of the individual, and its presentation of *la langue* as a kind of psychological manifestation of collective uniformity," offers us "a theory of languages which explicitly mirrored the ideally integrated, stable community which the nation-state would have liked to be" (Harris, 1980, p. 157). In other words, the "language myth" which is at the heart of orthodox linguistic theory—including the Hallidayan "systemic functional" approach on which CDA so relies—has its roots in a particular ideological conception which now comes back to haunt us in the guise of the "structuralist–constructivist" view of discourse.

We do not wish to deny the practical usefulness, within certain limits, of methods and insights from "segregational" linguistics. But to take the assumptions and results of such practices as a general model or theory of communication is to put ourselves at some distance from the sources, springs, and dynamic of communicative activity. In particular, the segregational approach forces the analyst to foreclose on the novelty of actual, conscious communicative behavior by forcing what is being said and done now into categories derived from a certain way of looking at what was said and done previously.[16]

The only alternative to the segregational account of language is, as Harris (1981) argued, an "integrational" one whose main principles are as follows:

> First and foremost, an integrational linguistics must recognise that human beings inhabit a communicational space which is not neatly compartmentalised into language and non-language ... It renounces in advance the possibility of setting up systems of forms and meanings which will "account for" a central core of linguistic behaviour irrespective of the situational and communicational purposes involved. (p. 165)

The point of departure for such an integrational approach to communication is not, then, the mythical "linguistic system" in the shape of a "code," a "language," a "discourse type," or "genre," but is "the individual linguistic act in its communicational setting" (Harris, 1981, p. 166).[17] It is not "the language" or "linguistic system" which determines the possibilities of linguistic expression on the part of the communicators, rather it is the following:

> ... language is continuously created by the interaction of individuals in specific communicational situations. It is this interaction which confers relevance on the participants' past experience with words, and not, as orthodox linguistics would have us believe, past experience (that is to say, mastery of "the language") which determines the communicational possibilities of their present interaction. (Harris, 1981, p. 166)

Of course, there exists "a fund of past linguistic experience" (Harris, 1981, p. 86) on which participants may, or must draw, but "from an integrational perspective" the key thing is not this fund as such but "the individual's adaptive use of it to meet the communicational requirements of the present", a use which "is — and can only be — manifest in the communication situation itself" (Harris, 1981, p. 187).

This integrational focus on "the individual linguistic act in its communicational setting" is not an empiricist's paradise; it does not at all negate the social character of communicative acts but it makes us think about their sociality in different terms. To start with, it makes us look for and try to understand communication there where it is actually taking place, where individuals

---

[19]In this context, we note Vološinov's (1973) critique of the "abstract objectivism" of structuralist linguistics: "Language as a stable system of normatively identical forms is merely a scientific abstraction, productive only in connection with certain particular practical and theoretical goals" (p. 98). To which he added the following: "This abstraction is not adequate to the concrete reality of language" (p. 98). Unfortunately, linguists who have appealed to Vološinov (including, ironically, the pioneers of CL and CDA) have unfortunately ignored the overall thrust of his critique, in particular his appeal for a "re-examination ... of language forms in their usual linguistic presentation" (1973, p. 96).

[20]Again, we note a parallel with Vološinov's (1973) own position that "the actual reality of language-speech" is "the social event of verbal interaction implemented in an utterance or utterances" (p. 94).

are not social cyphers, sociological variables, or "mere figureheads" (Harris, 1996, p. 62), whose utterances display and combine elements of the "code" or "discourse type," but real historical individuals going about some business. It makes us realize that communication is conscious human conduct taking place in definite circumstances for which the participants are responsible, and, in varying degrees, accountable, and that making sense of the communicative conduct of a particular individual involves nothing less than trying to figure out what they are up to, what the real and potential impact of their conduct on us and others might be, and what their motives and purposes are in relation to whatever is at stake in the business at hand. And, after all, it is only when we look at things this way that we are able to pass judgment on what they say, sometimes hastily, sometimes carefully, but always fallibly, as "stupid," "irrelevant," "truthful," "insulting," "banal," or "inspiring," and so forth. The theoretical elucidation of communication seen from this perspective is not about boiling particular utterances, texts, and documents down to some mythical residue of stable and constantly reproducible forms and meanings but about finding and understanding the distinctive contribution that the relevant parties make by their situated communicative conduct to a developing sphere of activity or engagement. This means finding ways to discover the relevant factual relations—the interconnections, transitions, and contradictions—between the communicative conduct of the communicators and everything else that is going on in the developing and changing "integrated continuum" of practices "which is itself the sole source of signification" (Harris, 1996, p. 164). If, therefore, the identification and interpretation of communicatively significant behavior is dependent on factual questions about the people communicating, what they are up to, and what they believe, then we cannot draw a principled, generally valid dividing line between linguistic form and meaning on the one hand and context on the other. In that case, the theoretical rationale for segregational linguistics, with its systems of codes and rules, disappears. And from that point of view it is simply a mistake to think that we can do justice to the sociality of communicative processes and practices—including their role in "the reproduction of relations of power" (Fairclough) more specifically—by reducing them to the elements of an already given "code."

It might be objected that modern linguistic theory has shown itself more than willing to take into account the role of what is referred to as "context" as a factor in communication. However, more often than not, context and language are seen as two separately identifiable spheres which then "interact" in some way so that the "code" is more or less determinable in isolation and is then put to use in context.[18] "What these models need to safeguard at all costs," as Harris (1996, p. 156), put it, "is the proposition that the same sign can appear in indefinitely many different

---

[21]Furthermore, see Harris (1996, p. 147) on the "insurmountable" difficulties posed by what he called "weak segregationism," that is the view that "the relevant communicational unit is not the sign as defined by the linguistic code but, in practice, the sign-in-its-context."

contexts without losing its identity." The integrational position, by contrast, is that "there is no sign without a context, and contexts are not given in advance. Signs, in short, are not waiting to be 'used:' they are created in and by the act of communication" (Harris, 1996, p. 6).

CONCLUSION

We have argued that there are flaws in CDA's conception of discourse and its social role, which result from adopting the abstract and one-sided account of linguistic communication offered by "segregational" linguistics, and, in particular, the Hallidayan "systemic functional" paradigm. But our quarrel with Fairclough and CDA over what discourse is and how to give an account of it has implications beyond the realm of linguistic description and methodology. Although Harris has clearly brought out the negative influence of segregational assumptions on the development of linguistic science, we have been concerned here with the damage these assumptions cause to our understanding of social action and the possibilities for social change when they are converted into a way of tackling ideology. If communicative processes are a dialectically integrated and differentiated dimension of social practice as a whole, then adopting a segregational approach to discourse necessarily entails a view of the dynamic of the social process which is distorted beyond recognition by the need to make that process fit with the properties of "discourse" as that approach sees them. The CDA position that language is "perhaps the primary medium of social control and power" (Fairclough, 1989, p. 3) is more a reading back of its own ideological orientation, imported from linguistics, into the social process, than the result of careful exploration of communicative processes in today's world.

In one sense, CDA damns itself in two ways: first, by the abyss between its conception of language and power and the violent reality of the exercise of power in the world today, and second, by its manifest irrelevance to the actual practices of political criticism and oppositional action which spring up, irrepressible, in every corner of that world. The devastating critiques of the political process, of corporate power, of military action, and of the workings of ideology to be found in a Chomsky, Pilger, Monbiot, Said, or even a Michael Moore, to mention only those writers who have some success in the mainstream, owe nothing to the methods of CDA. Here there is no "linguistic analysis," or any preconception about the "constitutive role of discourse." Instead, there is a passionately engaged process of discovery and exposure of the workings of power based on diligent exploration and informed piecing together and analysis of the facts and circumstances, making sense of the significance and distinctive contributions of documents, speeches, and other records of communicative practices in the light of their emerging insights into the sequence, causes, logic, and meaning of a series of events. Here there is no "discourse analysis" in the CDA sense but there is plenty of careful, informed, and critical examination of the communicative activities and conduct of those whose job it is to "manufacture consent" or to organize a war in secret. There is more to be learnt from their work about the ideological role of communicative practices, as well as about the practices of opposition, critique, and resistance, than in all the works of the CDA tradition.

And yet, as academics, we cannot afford to ignore the role of the "linguistic turn" in influencing, to one degree or another, the intellectual climate and research culture within the academy and beyond. The impression one can get from CDA that the pressing issues, problems, and crises we face in the world today do not require detailed and conscientious empirical investigation or knowledge and expertise in the relevant spheres but can be understood and addressed using a toolkit taken from segregational linguistics is an impression that we wish to vigorously contest.

Our second article (Collins & Jones, in press) takes the argument further and from a different angle in connection with the analysis of a particular case of "oppositional discourse" which arose during a political conflict over socialist housing policy in the labor and trade union movement in Glasgow, Scotland, in 1984.

REFERENCES

Abercrombie, N., Hill, S., Turner, B. S. (1980). *The dominant ideology thesis*. London: Allen & Unwin.
Anderson, P. (1976). *Considerations on Western Marxism*. London: NLB.
Anderson, P. (1983). *In the tracks of historical materialism*. London: Verso.
Bennett, T. (2003). *Formalism and Marxism*. London: Routledge.
Chouliaraki, L., & Fairclough, N. (1999). *Discourse in late modernity. Rethinking critical discourse analysis*. Edinburgh, Scotland: Edinburgh University Press.
Collins, C. (1999a). *Language, ideology and social consciousness: Developing a sociohistorical approach*. Aldershot, England: Ashgate.
Collins, C. (1999b) Applying Bakhtin in urban studies: The failure of community participation in the Ferguslie Park Partnership. *Urban Studies, 36*, 73–90.
Collins, C. (2000). Developing the linguistic turn in urban studies: Language, context and political economy. *Urban Studies, 37*, 2027–2043.
Collins, C. (2003). Critical psychology and contemporary struggles against neo-liberalism: Some suggestions based on experience from the west of Scotland. *Annual Review of Critical Psychology, 3*, 26–48.
Eagleton, T. (1991). *Ideology: An introduction*. London: Verso.
Fairclough, N. (1989). *Language and power*. London: Longman.
Fairclough, N. (1992). *Discourse and social change*. Oxford, England: Polity Press.
Fairclough, N. (1995). *Critical discourse analysis: The critical study of language*. London: Longman.
Fairclough, N. (2000). *New labour, new language?* London: Routledge & Kegan Paul.
Fairclough, N. (2001a). *Language and power* (2nd ed.). London: Longman/Pearson.
Fairclough, N. (2001b). Critical discourse analysis as a method in social scientific research. In R. Wodak & M. Meyer (Eds.), *Methods of critical discourse analysis* (pp. 121–138). London: Sage.
Fairclough, N., & Graham, P. (2002). Marx and discourse analysis: Genesis of a critical method. *Estudios de Sociolinguistica, 3*, 185–230.
Fowler, R., Hodge, B., Kress, G., & Trews, T. (Eds.). (1979). *Language and control*. London: Routledge & Kegan Paul.

Fowler, R., & Kress, G. (1979). Critical linguistics. In R. Fowler, B. Hodge, G. Kress, & T. Trew (Eds.), *Language and control.* London: Routledge & Kegan Paul.

Gunson, D., & Collins, C. (1997). From the "I" to the "We": Discourse ethics, identity and the pragmatics of partnership in the west of Scotland' *Communication Theory, 7,* 277–300.

Harris, R. (1980). *The language-makers.* London: Duckworth.

Harris, R. (1981). *The language myth.* London: Duckworth.

Harris, R. (1996). *Signs, language and communication.* London: Routledge & Kegan Paul.

Hutton, C. M. (1990). *Abstraction and instance.* Oxford, England: Pergamon.

Ilyenkov, E. V. (1982). *The dialectics of the abstract and the concrete in Marx's 'capital.'* Moscow: Progress Publishers.

Ilyenkov, E. V. (1997). *Dialektika abstraktnogo i konkretnago v nauchno-teoreticheskom myshlenii* [The dialectics of the abstract and the concrete in theoretical–scientific thinking]. Moscow: Rosspen.

Jones, P. E. (2001). Cognitive linguistics and the Marxist approach to ideology. In R. Dirven, B. Hawkins, & E. Sandikcioglu (Eds.), *Language and ideology. Volume 1: Theoretical cognitive approaches* (pp. 227–251). Amsterdam: Benjamins.

Jones, P. E. (2004a). Discourse and the materialist conception of history: Critical comments on critical discourse analysis. *Historical Materialism, 12,* 97–125.

Jones, P. E. (2004b). Discourse, social change, and the CHAT tradition. Review of Collins (1999a). *Mind, Culture, and Activity, 11,* 170–172.

Jones, P. E. (XXXX). Why there is no such thing as critical discourse analysis.

Marx, K., & Engels, F. (1969). *Selected works in three volumes. Volume 1.* Moscow: Progress.

Scott, J. C. (1990). *Domination and the arts of resistance.* London: Yale University Press.

Thompson, E. P (1978). *The poverty of theory and other essays.* London: Merlin.

Thompson, J. B. (1984). *Studies in the theory of ideology.* Oxford, England: Polity Press.

Thompson, J. B. (1990). *Ideology and modern culture.* Oxford, England: Polity Press.

Trew, T. (1979). "What the papers say": Linguistic variation and ideological difference. In R. Fowler, B. Hodge, G. Kress, & T. Trew (Eds.), *Language and control.* London: Routledge & Kegan Paul.

van Dijk, T. A. (1993). Principles of critical discourse analysis. *Discourse and Society, 4,* 249–283.

Vološinov, V. N. (1973). *Marxism and the philosophy of language.* New York: Seminar Press.

Widdowson, H. G. (1998). The theory and practice of critical discourse analysis. *Applied Linguistics, 19,* 136–151.

Wodak, R., & Meyer, M. (2001). *Methods of critical discourse analysis.* London: Sage.

Analysis of Discourse as "a Form of History Writing": A Critique of Critical Discourse Analysis and an Illustration of a Cultural–Historical Alternative

Chik Collins
University of Paisley, Scotland

Peter E. Jones
Sheffield Hallam University, England

This article, the second in a pair of collaborative articles (see Jones & Collins, this issue), extends our critique of an ongoing attempt, in the tradition of "Critical Linguistics" (CL) and "Critical Discourse Analysis" (CDA), to link the tools of linguistics and discourse analysis to a critical theory of power and ideology. We are entirely supportive of the idea of critically analyzing ideology in real-life situations, of analyzing it through engagement with language-use or discourse, and of using this as a significant element in a method for the study of social change. But we argue that the CL-CDA project is deeply problematic. Drawing briefly on the tradition of cultural–historical and activity theory, we outline an alternative method for the critical analysis of discourse. We illustrate this with a case study of "oppositional discourse."

LANGUAGE, CONTEXT, AND HISTORY

Roger Fowler was perhaps the key figure in the creation of the CL-CDA school (Fowler, Hodge, Kress, & Trew, 1979). Yet in an essay first published in 1987, he ex-

---

Correspondence should be addressed to Chik Collins, Politics and Sociology, School of Social Sciences, University of Paisley, Paisley, Renfrewshire, PA1 2BE, Scotland, E-mail: chik.collins@paisley.ac.uk

pressed frustration with its development (Fowler, 1996). He seemed particularly frustrated by the reluctance to engage with "the question of history and context" (Fowler et al., 1996, p. 9). On the one hand, practitioners avowed that linguistic significance was heavily dependent on context. On the other, actual analyses treated context at best sketchily, and tended to assume that readers already knew it and shared the analyst's view of it. The troubling implication was that "students" were "likely to believe that the descriptive tools of linguistics provide some privilege of access to the interpretation of the text." But this is, of course, not the case, and so students might end up "not knowing where to start," and perhaps even come to believe that linguistics really is, after all, a "discovery procedure" (Fowler, 1996, pp. 9–10). Here Fowler's (1996) frustration became tangible. In the future, it would be necessary "to take a *professionally responsible attitude* towards the analysis of context" (p. 10; our emphasis). This might usefully entail seeing CL "as a form of history-writing" (Fowler et al., 1979, p. 10). To "understand the text," analysts would have to "bring to it relevant experience of discourse and of context" (Fowler, 1996, p. 9). "Linguistic description" would then come "at a later stage, as a means of getting some purchase on the significances that one has heuristically assigned to the text" (Fowler, 1996, p. 9).

Fowler's essay was republished, only "slightly modified," in 1996 (p. 13, no. 1). But there was no suggestion that problems previously diagnosed had been addressed, even with the appearance of two of the most influential works in CDA (Fairclough, 1989, 1992). Indeed, the latter seem rather to exemplify these problems (Collins, 1999).

In this respect, the whole CDA enterprise remains deeply problematic. It claims that communicative practices play a crucial role in processes of social and political change, yet, at the same time, it eschews the kind of engagement with "history and context" which might allow that claim to be demonstrated.

In this light, one can understand Fowler's frustration. What he seemed to be saying was that there is no method—critical or otherwise—by which we can grasp linguistic significance, or the role of discourse in processes of social and political change, outside of a concrete understanding of the interconnected circumstances in and through which it arises. And in this he seemed to be pointing toward something more profound than the idea that discourse should be situated or embedded in its context after the event—so to speak—as if the relation between the two were one of interaction. This manner of thinking seems characteristic not just of attempts to connect linguistics to "the social," but also of parallel developments in other disciplines—notably psychology (see Stetsenko & Arievitch, 2004a). Such thinking certainly represents progress in these fields, but it hardly encapsulates the real problem, which is to grasp discourse itself as an integral moment in the generative process of social life of particular communities in particular times and places. How, then, might we address this problem of "history and context" more effectively?

FROM CONTEXT TO CONCRETENESS

A perspective that perhaps helps concretize the kind of thinking Fowler was developing is to be found in the cultural–historical and activity theory tradition, which emerged in Soviet psychology—in the writings of historical figures such as Vygotsky, Leont'ev, Luria, and Ilyenkov—and which is best represented in the present in contributions now emerging from writers such as Stetsenko and Arievitch (2004a, 2004b), and Sawchuk, Duarte, and Elhamoumi (2006).[1] This tradition is rooted in historical materialism, and is geared toward grasping social phenomena concretely, in their "internal relations" to other phenomena in a developing system. Thus, Ilyenkov (1982) stated the following:

> To comprehend a phenomenon means to establish its place and role in the concrete system of interacting phenomena in which it is necessarily realized, and to find out precisely those traits which make it possible for the phenomenon to play this role .... To comprehend a phenomenon means to discover the mode of its origin, the rule according to which the phenomenon emerges with necessity rooted in the concrete totality of conditions .... (p. 177)

Similarly, for Stetsenko and Arievitch (2004a), grasping a phenomenon as "sociocultural and historical" means grasping it as "produced from within, out of, and as driven by the logic of evolving activity that connect individuals to the world, to other people and to themselves" (p. 486).

This perspective seems to connect with Fowler's concerns, and to suggest a similar order for the analysis of discursive materials. For it too points to the engagement with discourse, after some preliminary, or "heuristic," engagement, as "a form of history writing." It points to the necessity of proceeding to grasp the "logic of evolving activity" and the ongoing development in a "concrete system of interacting phenomena," before returning to the analysis of discourse in a new light.

In this perspective, it is precisely the fact that discourse is produced in and through the "logic of evolving activity" that gives it such relevance to the study of social change. For, as an integral product of the real historical development of particular communities, discourse reveals traces of that development, of its twists and turns, and significant moments of change and reconstitution. Such traces provide vital prompts and clues to the researcher, who can work from them to begin to reconstruct, and hopefully also to grasp, the historical developments from within, and out of, which particular uses of language were generated. In this way, research can begin "heuristically" from discursive processes and proceed to generate an account of a larger pattern of sociohistorical development which is in turn the key to, in Ilyenkov's terms, the comprehension of those same discursive processes.

---

[1]We have ourselves sought to make some contributions (Collins, 1999, 2000; Jones 2001, 2004).

We can call this a method of discourse analysis. But we use this term in its broadest sense, as a general orientation or approach. It does not entail an attempt to specify a determinate methodology, even less a procedural checklist of linguistic features which might be of significance. Such an attempt would seem out of step with the very nature of critical engagement with language use. Toolan (1996) put it as follows: "it is open to question whether a perspective so definitionally sensitive to the varying requirements of each new communicational situation could yield anything so determinate as a methodology" (p. 22).

In what follows, we seek to provide a substantial illustration—although given constraints of space not a fully detailed demonstration—of such an approach.[2] We begin with a document produced by an official in the Housing Department of Glasgow District Council—the Labour Party-controlled municipal authority for the city of Glasgow, Scotland—in 1984 (Webster, 1984). It deals with issues relating to the future of the Council's provision of rented housing in the city. The "housing question" in Glasgow is long-standing and controversial. Indeed, it is understood that decisions in the 1984 to 1985 period established a longer-term policy agenda at national level. The document enunciates the justifications offered for those decisions.

"THE SOCIALIST CASE FOR COMMUNITY OWNERSHIP"

Let us begin with a preliminary, or heuristic, treatment of this document. It is headed "Briefing Paper" and dated August 21, 1984. It carries the initials DW, and is titled "The socialist case for community ownership." It begins as follows:

> Cooperatives ... have held a central place in the socialist tradition. Opposition has nevertheless been expressed to Glasgow District Council's proposals to transfer some housing schemes to par value cooperatives, on the ground that such a move is equivalent to "privatization" as practiced by the Thatcher government. The purpose of this article is to draw together relevant socialist writing so as to make the socialist case for the community ownership scheme. (Webster, 1984, p. 1)

The document runs to 11½ of A4 size, and quotes extensively from a range of historical and then contemporary sources to make this "socialist case." It begins by stressing the "central role" of "the co-operative idea" in "the development of socialism," and "its validity as part of the socialist tradition" (Webster, 1984, p. 1). It reports achievements of "worker-directed and worker-led" housing cooperatives in Scotland in the mid-19th century, and then states the following: "Perhaps surprisingly, co-operatives subsequently played no role in socialist housing policy in Brit-

---

[2]A more detailed manuscript is available from the authors.

ain until the 1970s. This was in complete contrast to the position in Germany ... and especially in Scandinavia" (Webster, 1984, p. 2). In the latter case, it is suggested, housing provision has been marked by greater "sensitivity ... to the needs and preferences of consumers than has been the case in Britain," particularly sensitivity to "the views of women" (Webster, 1984, p. 2).

Growing interest in cooperatives in Labour Party thinking about housing is then outlined, with "the logical conclusion" of such developments being, in the words of a 1981 Party "Discussion Document," "full devolution" of housing provision from elected municipal authorities "to a self-governing housing co-operative" such as "a par value co-operative" in which "the co-operative's property is collectively owned by its members but they have no individual financial stake" (Allaun et al., cited in Webster, 1984, p. 4).

Such cooperatives are presented as part of the "renewal of socialism in the 1980s." This "renewal," it is argued, requires socialists to confront an "important weakness" in the "bureaucratic character of welfare state services." In what has become "almost a new orthodoxy," "statism," "centralization and bureaucracy," are being counterposed to "a revival of the ideas of community and neighbourhood" as the basis for socialist policies. In this context, community ownership of housing is "part of the vital process of renewal in British socialism" (Webster, 1984, pp. 4–5).

The key sources disseminating such thinking are given as the journals *Marxism Today*, *The New Statesman*, and *The New Socialist* (Webster, 1984, p. 6). Commentators are cited along the following lines:

> Ordinary people are quite right to be up in arms about the bureaucratic maze they are forced to fight their way through in order to obtain the welfare benefits to which they are entitled [or] the housing transfer they need ... It is vital for the labour movement to acknowledge openly that the welfare system as presently organised can be oppressive ... to poor people ... Otherwise the whole socialist principle of the welfare society will be discredited, and we shall continue to lose ground to the populist right. (Hain & Hebditch, cited in Webster, 1984, p. 7)

> It is not socialist, nor ... is it popular to create centralised institutions which are run as autocratically in the public sector as in any private sector. ... We should develop new and more flexible forms of social ownership ... We should break down concentrations of power wherever they arise ... and make authority less remote and more manageable. (Gould, cited in Webster, 1984, p. 7)

In this light, "revival of the ideas of community and neighbourhood" are seen as the basis for "the renewal of socialism in the 1980s" (Webster, 1984, pp. 4–5). Their relevance is seen in their capacity to reconnect people to socialist ideals of mutuality, and, quoting Radice, "sharing in common purposes, activities and values" (Radice, cited in Webster, 1984, p. 9).

The argument then concludes as follows: "It is ... obvious that the general line of argument applies strongly to council housing and to developments such as the Community Ownership scheme" (Webster, 1984, p. 10). Provision of rented housing by local councils is marked by "paternalistic attitudes" and its providers "have not been sympathetic to the needs of the large and increasingly self-confident communities"[8] (Morrel, Reid, & Townsend, cited in Webster, 1984, p. 10). Labour administration of housing is "often bureaucratic, inefficient, authoritarian and insensitive"[9] (Hindess, cited in Webster, 1984, p. 11). Community ownership represents the best available socialist idea for confronting these problems (Webster, 1984, pp. 10–11).

THE ORDER OF DISCOURSE ANALYSIS

How might we begin to make sense of this discourse, and to evaluate its role in the relevant political actions and events with which it was bound up? Starting "heuristically," it is apparent that the housing question in the city is highly emotive. Some are proposing a significant departure in the form of transfer of council housing to "par value cooperatives" in a "community ownership scheme." The proposers feel the need to justify themselves in terms of socialist principles—thus the title. However, its very formulation seems to suggest that at some stage, the scheme has not been explicitly informed by such principles. How in fact did the proposal emerge?

The "case" as it is then outlined reveals clear traces of the history of housing provision in Glasgow—and Scotland and the United Kingdom generally. It indicates the leading role of local government (or councils) in providing rented housing on a mass scale. It also points to dissatisfaction with that form of provision, and to different perspectives on how it might be addressed—including attempts to develop alternatives. It then testifies to the advent of Thatcherite neo-liberalism, and the attempt to harness the aforementioned dissatisfaction to its privatizing agenda.

These seem to be the broad outlines of the historical process that produces "the socialist case for community ownership." If we are to comprehend that discourse, its process of production, and its role in an evolving process of social change, then we need to reconstruct that history in more detail—first in its relation to the city of Glasgow, but also in view of broader political and economic factors.

On the basis of such intercourse with concrete historical processes, we can attempt critically to grasp the contribution of specific discursive practices to the ongoing process. Such attempts will of course be contestable, and open to revision in light of new evidence. Yet outside of such intercourse, they will not meaningfully be possible. And in turn, their contestation will intrinsically involve such intercourse. For to contest an attempt to analyze the discourse will be to contest the analysis of the contribution of the discourse, which will be to contest the reconstruction of the "evolving activity" of which the discourse is part.

"THE LOGIC OF EVOLVING ACTIVITY"

Council Housing and its Problems

Provision of rented housing on a mass scale by elected local councils developed initially in Britain in the aftermath of World War I. It emerged through the struggles of working people against private landlordism, and in pursuit of decent, affordable housing for those who had endured the war. The working class of Glasgow, suffering particularly dreadful housing conditions, were to the fore in these struggles. Yet, in the interwar period, only a very limited number of houses were actually built, and these remained for the most part out of the reach of the ordinary working class. It was in the aftermath of World War II that the labor and trade union movement made council housing central to the British welfare state. It was to become particularly important in Scotland. By the late 1970s, more than a half of all Scotland's housing was in the public rented sector, compared with less than a third in England and Wales. In Glasgow, the figure was approaching two thirds (O'Carroll, 1996, p. 17). At this point, one moderate Scottish commentator was able to speak confidently, if not unconditionally, of "the virtually heroic building achievements of our local authorities" (Cook, 1975, p. 335).

Yet the development of this system threw up a range of problems, and Glasgow's were particularly acute. Post-World War II, the Council wished to rehouse its working class in new estates on the city's peripheries. But central government wanted to disperse industry and population to "new towns." A struggle ensued, with the city finally emerging the loser. Large peripheral schemes were built, but many inhabitants were also dispersed. The delay proved crucial. It increased pressure on the council to build its peripheral estates quickly, and to neglect the provision of services and amenities, which it was hoped could be delivered at a later stage as a by-product of economic growth. The actual outcome was economic slowdown, and a continuing lack of basic services and amenities (Gibb, 1989, p. 161). Dissatisfaction grew, and by the early 1970s, a third of the inhabitants of these estates were asking to be housed elsewhere (Cable, 1975, p. 243).

Moreover, council housing was centralized and bureaucratic. It left little scope for inputs from tenants. Typically, its administration reflected the prejudices of "urban gatekeepers." Households would be allocated to areas on the basis of judgements of their moral worth. On this basis, much of the least desirable housing had been allowed to develop into "areas of intense social stress" (Cable, 1975, p. 242).

By the later 1960s, then, it was already clear that previous housing "solutions" had bequeathed significant problems. As the postwar social democratic consensus broke down, and as government moved to embrace monetarism, these problems were to intensify. With the election of the Conservatives to the UK Parliament in 1979, they were to become much worse.

The Impact of Neo-Liberalism and the Council's "Community Ownership Scheme"

For the Thatcherite neo-liberals, council housing was the basis of "municipal socialism," and was implicated in the kinds of working class identity which had challenged the neo-liberal policies of the Conservatives under Edward Heath in the early 1970s (Foster & Woolfson, 1986). Its dismantling was a key priority. Post-1979, central control of housing finance was used to reduce, and ultimately halt, new council building. Rent levels were forced up by reducing available subsidies. At the same time, councils were starved of the funds required to carry out repairs and improvements. Crucially, government also legislated to give tenants the "right to buy" their council houses at heavily discounted rates. This was to mean councils losing their most desirable and easiest to manage houses, and retaining an increasingly "residualized" and deteriorating stock tenanted by the poorest households. Across Britain, this was to prove the largest privatization of the Thatcher years (Kemp, 1992, p. 70). By the mid-1980s, commentators were writing about the resulting "housing crisis" (Malpass, 1986).

Glasgow was a particular target for the government. Its council was dominated by the Labour Party and it was reputedly the largest landlord in Western Europe. It had been at the forefront of the movement that had created council housing, and its working class had been prominent in forcing Heath's "u-turn" (Foster & Woolfson, 1986). The city's peripheral estates of the 1950s were now requiring major investment. Yet the council's borrowing limit (controlled by central government) was being seriously reduced. Cuts in subsidies also meant that, even with large rent increases, income was insufficient to fund essential repairs. At the same time, however, the council was given increased scope to spend on improving housing outwith the council sector.

In June 1983, Thatcher's Conservatives were elected for a further term, with a crushing parliamentary majority. The city's Director of Housing, Paul Mugnaioni, now proposed that by transferring some houses into independent "community ownership," it would be possible to divert to them spending permitted outwith the council sector. This idea was developed along the lines of par value cooperatives (mentioned earlier). Any transfer would need the approval of the Conservative government. But, this did not seem impossible, for the scheme had an obvious appeal for those who disliked municipal housing. A specific proposal was elaborated, which was to establish three to four small cooperatives in the first instance. The scheme would, however, also require the backing of the city's District Labour Party and of the trade unions representing the council's many housing workers.

The Opposition and the Response

For many in the city's labor movement, with their attachment to some idea of socialism, the "community ownership scheme" seemed incongruous. For some it was an unwelcome diversion from the need to secure improvements across the council's stock, and for others it looked worryingly like complicity with the aims of Thatcher's government. This held true even among those on the left who were most critical of council housing. This can be seen in the logic of the "community action" movement which developed from the late 1960s. It too sought to challenge the bureaucratic and paternalistic nature of the welfare state, and to transfer meaningful power out of the hands of the politicians and bureaucrats, and into the hands of local communities. But the "community action" critique did not advocate the dismantling of collective provision, or that community groups should assume the task of providing for themselves. In the words of Kirkwood, a Glasgow-based participant–observer of Glasgow's "rich crop of local action" in the early 1970s, this was seen as specifically "reactionary." The need was to defend and democratize large-scale collective provision (Kirkwood, 1975, p. 96). This kind of thinking clearly remained influential a decade later. In this light, the whole "community ownership" idea looked as if it might be "suffocated at birth" (Keating, 1985).

We also need to recall the broader—and highly charged—political dynamic. The 1984 to 1985 Miners' Strike—the definitive political confrontation of the Thatcher years—was in progress, and its outcome was still in the balance. At the same time, a number of other Labour councils were seeking publicly to mobilize opposition to the government. Glasgow was not. Instead, when the Conservatives were challenging the very basis of the welfare state, and of the labor and trade union movement itself, the proposal seemed to be in line with the government's demunicipalization agenda. This made many in the city's labor movement quite uneasy.

In this light, the promoters turned to a council official, David Webster (DW), to "sell" their proposal. This was to mean justifying the scheme not only as a defensibly "socialist" response to the Conservative attacks, but as one that was superior to other "socialist" attempts to defend the existing system. Webster's "briefing paper," outlined earlier, was circulated in August 1984, and its "case" projected in the city's labor and trade union movement by sympathetic elements.

Having now sought to reintegrate that "case" in "the concrete system of interacting phenomena" of which it was a vital part, we can begin to grasp something very fundamental about it. Although the "case" as stated may have appeared to reflect the influence of the "community action" critique of paternalism and bureaucracy, the actual emergence of the "community ownership" proposal reflected precisely the paternalistic and bureaucratic system that the "community action" movement had sought to challenge. The proposal was not a reflection of any demands from local groups for independence from their council landlord. It had not begun from socialist ideas and commitments and resulted in a specific proposal. Rather, it had emerged from the upper echelons of the bureaucracy, had met with opposition grounded in socialist values, and the bureaucracy had in turn sought to meet that opposition on its own grounds (Holmes, 1990). There was, in other words, a serious gap between what was being justified, and its justification. Crucially, this is something we would not typically have found through CDA, because the "concrete system of interacting phenomena" would not have been reconstructed sufficiently to see it.

CHANGE

So what part did this discourse play in the subsequent unfolding of events? Let us "fast forward" a little to see how they did unfold.

Glasgow

Within a few months of the production of "the socialist case," the District Labour Party and the principal unions had dropped their opposition. Three small areas of housing had been identified, and tenants were brought on board with the promise of substantial investment. A specific proposal was now put to central government. But although the latter approved the principle of "community ownership," they rejected the idea of the cooperatives as independent entities. Instead, it was proposed, they should follow a different model—one already well known in Glasgow.

This model had emerged in Glasgow in the wake of the 1974 Housing Act. The latter provided generous subsidies to "voluntary" housing associations, which registered with a government agency (the Housing Corporation in Scotland—HCiS), to acquire, improve, and let housing. In Glasgow, these organizations took the form of "Community-Based Housing Associations," which became active in the remaining Victorian tenements of the inner city. However, these were not quite the spontaneous outgrowths of the city's "rich crop of local action" that the name might suggest. They were in effect the "tool of central government" (Matheson, 1976, p. 66), and their only real accountability was to central government itself.

Now the government proposed that, rather than creating "independent" cooperatives, the new organizations should register with the HCiS, and become, in effect, housing associations, funded and controlled by central government. This, in fact, was a possibility that had earlier been considered by the council, and explicitly ruled out (Holmes, 1990, pp. 32–33). Such bodies could not be justified in terms of socialist cooperation. Now, however, this objection was forgotten. It was left to the tenants in the three areas to decide whether to proceed on this basis. Holmes (1990) noted the following: "The only choice the tenants had was to accept the … funding with HCiS control and get their houses improved, or reject it and continue staying in damp, rundown hard to heat housing in a poor environment" (p. 34).

With this a clear precedent had been established for transfers to housing associations (although called "cooperatives") as a way of demunicipalizing council housing and placing it under central control. Yet the narratives of these new organizations remained along the previous lines: bold new experiments in grass roots activism, local communities breaking free from paternalism and bureaucracy to create a better future, a model to emulate. Glasgow rapidly proceeded to a second phase of transfers. Soon, it was being proposed that 25% of Glasgow's stock be transferred; 50% in the peripheral estates (Grieve, Clark, Finniston, & Karn, 1986).

Scotland

The significance of all of this was not lost on Conservative policy strategists. There were clear limits to the "right-to-buy" as a means of demunicipalizing housing stock; only a fraction of the total would ever be sold through it. As one government minister was to put it, "the next big push after the right to buy should be to get rid of the state as a big landlord" (Waldegrave, cited in Kemp, 1992, p. 68). Here, it seemed, was one potentially useful way of progressing that, and in Scotland it was to be taken up as a key part of the agenda for Thatcher's radical third term (beginning in 1987). The HCiS would be subsumed in a new organization (Scottish Homes) with the mission of driving tenure change. Such limited housing investment as there was to be would be used as a carrot to secure further transfers. The council stock would be allowed to deteriorate further, whereas rents would be forced up, so pushing remaining tenants ever more toward "the right to buy," transfer, or into owner occupation outwith the council stock.

Housing associations would also be subject to a new regime requiring a greater level of private finance. This would expose them to what the government called "the disciplines of the market" (Kemp, 1992, p. 68). It would also mean increasing rents and a new legal form of tenancy, both of which would bolster the previously declining private rented sector, which the Conservatives wished to revive.

In the event, however—as is typically the case with neo-liberal agendas—the government failed to achieve many of its stated aims. The private rented sector did not burgeon to the desired extent. Although changing in significant ways, housing associations were able to limit their exposure to "the discipline of the market." The scale of transfers from the council sector was much lower than had been hoped. But crucially, tenure change was very much the focus of policy and of debate, distracting attention from the continuing plight of the broader mass of council tenants. The result was that for a further decade, Glasgow, and Scotland as a whole, endured a massively damaging housing policy. In the various pockets of housing transferred, conditions improved markedly, whereas in the much broader council sector there were at best much more limited improvements and more generally continuing deterioration. The continuing upward pressure on rents worked to drive households with even modest levels of income into owner occupation. Thus, Murie (1996) put it as follows:

> The public rental sector in Scotland has changed it role from the mainstream sector housing the mass of the working population and families with children. It has become increasingly residualised, housing elderly persons, the long-term sick and disabled, and households not in employment with high dependency on benefits. (p. 60)

As the more desirable stock was sold, and as those with sufficient resources left, policy worked to concentrate the poorest, and most troubled, households in the least desirable areas. Communities became radically imbalanced and demoralized, with very low labor market participation, high rates of family breakdown, mass educational failure, and increasing drug use and associated criminality and incarceration. The basic fabric of social life in such areas—and Glasgow had a disproportionate share of them—began to come apart. Had one made this the aim of housing policy, one could scarcely have designed anything more effective.

DISCOURSE AND CHANGE

If these were the changes, then what part did "the socialist case for community ownership" play in their unfolding? Here we return to the analysis of discourse, but not as some abstraction; not as a "discourse sample" treated in separation from "the concrete system of interacting phenomena" of which it was a vital part. We return to it in its most vital connections in an ongoing process of social change. In doing so, we do not find that this use of language was unimportant. Rather we are able to see just how important it was; perhaps more important than even those who would want to make the case for the great importance of language might have dared to suggest. For the political opposition, to say nothing of various legal and financial difficulties, which faced the "community ownership" proposals in 1984 and 1985, was very substantial. There was a very real prospect, clearly reflected in the contemporary commentary, that the whole idea could have been peremptorily smothered. To ordinary Labour Party members, disposing of hard-won municipal housing seemed an anathema. To one of the main trade unions concerned, it was as follows: "outright privatization which must be opposed in line with national policy." Yet, mobilizing "the socialist case for community ownership," the proponents were able to overturn this decision. At a specially convened general meeting of the union, "community ownership" was duly recognized as "a variety of co-operative and common ownership in line with the traditional aspirations of the Labour movement" (Keating, 1985, p. 2058). A similar view was secured in the District Labour Party (Holmes, 1990, p. 29). These decisions were vital in ensuring that the scheme survived in the early stages and that its proponents were able to develop it to the point where it could be sustained by its own inherent momentum; even when the gap between its ostensible justification and its actual form would be all too apparent.

When we also learn that some of those personnel most vital in the incubation of the scheme were soon to leave the council to pursue careers in other pastures, then the importance of winning this contest for legitimacy in the early stages becomes even more apparent (Holmes, 1990, p. 38). Significantly, the key individual behind the scheme, the Director of Housing, left the council to set up Quality Street—a private residential lettings company backed by the Nationwide Building Society, and designed to exploit the new potentialities for private landlordism that the Conservatives were creating.[3]

In this light, the real importance of "the socialist case for community ownership" becomes apparent. Projected in the debates in the city's labor movement, it played a required role in ensuring that the scheme was not blocked in the early stages by an opposition articulating socialist values. Had the scheme been blocked, then it seems very likely that it would not have developed in the way that it did, and quite possible that it would not have developed further at all. The subsequent history of housing policy in Scotland might have been quite different.[4]

It also becomes apparent that the real danger in this situation, in ideological terms, came not straightforwardly from the neo-liberal right, but heavily mediated by the views of what was then called the "soft left" about how left politics had to change. In Scotland, and Glasgow in particular, familiar neo-liberal rhetoric was fairly easily penetrated—especially by those in the labor movement—and was deeply unpopular. What was rather more difficult to cope with was the discourse of the "soft left"associated with journals like *Marxism Today*, *The New Socialist*, and *The New Statesman*. Yet, as we have seen here, such discourse could easily be harnessed to the justification of policies compatible with the aims of the Conservatives. This "soft left" was itself actively promoting the "break down of concentrations of power" which the Conservatives sought; concentrations of power which needed to be galvanized if any kind of challenge to their policies were to be

---

[3]This is not suggestive of a deep commitment to the values of socialism.

[4]Crucially, the emerging tenure change agenda radically undermined the potential for the kind of movement that might have challenged the government's housing policies. Its impact was highly divisive, with small groups of tenants benefiting whereas the larger body of tenants continued to live with deteriorating conditions. Larger councils, particularly Glasgow, sought to transfer stock wherever possible, often becoming involved in micromanagement of local community organizations to head off protest and secure consent. All of this was deeply corrosive to the kind of trust and solidarity among tenants, and between tenants and the local authority, that would have been needed to project a challenge to government policy. Thus, although it was to prove possible in the years ahead to build a mass movement to defeat the "poll tax"—and ultimately to have Thatcher removed as Prime Minister—it was not possible to build on the success of this movement in building an effective challenge to her government's housing policies.

mounted. Were they to be broken down, then there would be less power that was even susceptible to democratic control, and the prospects for democracy would, as has proven to be the case, be significantly reduced.

A key failure of the forces opposing this seems to have been to misanalyze the transfer proposal, labeling it as "outright privatization" and as a "return to private landlordism." But this was too crude. A "par value cooperative" as conceived in the "community ownership scheme" did not represent an immediate "return to private landlordism." Whatever the merits of the original proposal, the real problem was that the scheme could too easily be manipulated to make it conform to another agenda. Along these lines, stock transfer was to become, post-1987, part of a broader transitional policy intended to shift the legal framework and rental market for housing so that the private rental sector would ultimately be able to reemerge as a significant player. By analyzing the threat of "private landlordism" as something more immediate than this, the opposition left themselves open to refutation, and to the accusation that they were opposing, on erroneous—perhaps even ideological—grounds, investment which "decent tenants" desperately needed, and which "no one had any right to deny them." A more careful analysis was required in this crucial debate, and in its absence the "socialist case for community ownership" created enough doubt and disorientation about what was at stake for the proposal to survive and proceed to the next stage.

Yet it is necessary to point out that the ideological case for the "community ownership scheme" would by no means have been the only weapon in the struggle to defeat the opposition. "Administrative" measures would almost certainly have played a role. With some parts of the labor movement beholden to the council for resources of one kind or another, key people could have been "called in" and "reminded of who their friends were."[5] Yet it seems improbable that such measures would have been enough to achieve the desired outcome. The ideological case, although it may not have itself been sufficient for that, seems clearly to have been necessary to it.

This, moreover, raises some very basic questions about the whole notion of "oppositional discourse." For it becomes apparent that the political nature of discourse cannot be evaluated by familiar forms of discourse analysis—even CDA—and certainly not by rendering abstract samples of discourse yet more abstract through textual and grammatical analysis, before later seeking to "contextualize" them. Only in seeking to grasp discourse concretely, in all its vital and internal connections with concrete social and historical processes, can an evaluation be made. At that point, it becomes meaningful to distinguish discourse that is genuinely oppositional, or even emancipatory, from that which is dominant or reactionary. For now the apparently oppositional ("socialist") discourse that we have here been analyzing seems clearly to fall into the reactionary category.

---

[5]Thanks to John Foster for important comments on this point.

POSTSCRIPT: HIDDEN CONNECTIONS OF CRITICAL DISCOURSE ANALYSIS

The Denouement: New Labour and Glasgow's "Whole Stock Transfer"

The implications of Glasgow's "community ownership" initiative were to prove even further reaching in the wake of the election of Tony Blair's New Labour to government in 1997, and the subsequent creation of the Scottish Parliament in 1999. The government quickly affirmed that the 'solution' to the crisis in Scotland's council housing lay primarily in transfers to "community ownership." In Glasgow's case, a "whole stock transfer" was proposed. By this time, 50% of all rental income was being used simply to service historic debts, leaving much too little for the required investment. The government proposed to alleviate this debt burden, but only if the council transferred its entire stock to a newly created body called Glasgow Housing Association. The new organization would then be in a position to raise private finance for investment. As in the mid-1980s, Glasgow tenants were presented with a "Hobson's choice," except now on a much larger scale. Yet it took an extensive publicity campaign, and a sustained offensive against oppositional groups, to secure, in March 2002, a modest "yes" vote in a ballot on the transfer proposals. Today the future of tenants in this former council stock is still far from clear. There is little sign that the new body is going to be able to deliver the required improvements in their housing.

Writing of this transfer, Sim (2004) noted the following:

> The scale of the transfer—the largest so far in the UK ...—represents a substantial tenure shift within Scotland, and is likely to pave the way for future transfers. Politically, the transfer is significant, as Glasgow City Council had perhaps been viewed as "old" Labour, yet it was able to agree to rid itself of its landlord role. (p. 5)

This is partly right. Glasgow is, after all, the city most prominent in the struggles that created council housing in the early 20th century, and the Labour Council's desire to be rid of its housing at the start of the 21st century is of great significance. But history shows that Labour in Glasgow in 1984 was anything but "old" in its attitudes. At this time, Glasgow's Labour Council played a crucial role in incubating the idea of stock transfer that was, by the end of the 1990s, to be at the heart of "new" Labour thinking. What links the two is their intimate connections with Thatcherite hostility to municipal housing—the first in helping to provide for its extension in Thatcher's third term and through the years of John Major's government, and the second in ensuring its continuation, toward logical completion, under New Labour through the Scottish Parliament.[6]

---

[6]Ironically, this institution was conceived as the expression of the nation's will in opposition to "Thatcherism."

The Hidden Connections of Critical Discourse Analysis

> Critical is used in the special sense of aiming to show up connections which may be hidden from people ... (Fairclough, 1989, p. 5).

The foregoing analysis raises significant questions for CDA. For historically it evolved out of the same political tendencies that in the 1980s provided the ideas and arguments which, although represented as a creative response to "Thatcherism," were in fact frequently complicit with the Conservatives' political aims.

Perhaps the clearest evidence of this is the link with the journal *Marxism Today*, and the thinking of Stuart Hall and Martin Jacques, and through this to the broader tradition of "Western Marxism." In the latter tradition, there is a rather simplistic inflation of the importance of ideology in "incorporating" subordinate groups into a dominant, or "hegemonic," value system. In the writings of Hall and Jacques (especially Hall & Jacques, 1983a, 1983b, 1983c, 1989; see also Hall, 1988), and in the journal *Marxism Today*, more generally, this tradition was expressed in the theory of "Thatcherism." "Thatcherism" was portrayed as a "novel and exceptional political force" Hall & Jacques, 1983a, p. 10) which was "shifting the political terrain" Hall & Jacques, 1983a, p. 13) and incorporating social groups across British society into "a new reactionary kind of common sense" Hall & Jacques, 1983a, p. 11) that was hostile to collective welfare. Politically, this meant the onset of "new times," involving "new realities," which called for "new politics;" a break from the ways of the "old left," and a reorientation to the politics of "hegemony" in "civil society" (see also Hall & Jacques, 1989; Hall, 1988).

Fairclough's CDA evolves manifestly from this intellectual current.[7] It was conceived as a contribution to the "new politics" it propounded; one of the key ways, indeed perhaps the most important way, in which critical social science could contribute to the unmasking of new right ideology in everyday lives.

Yet the "Thatcherism" perspective failed, and in its CDA manifestation has continued to fail, to engage with the actual evidence, which was that through the 1980s, the British people, and even less the people of Scotland, were clearly not being incorporated into some right ideological consensus. There was in fact a strengthening attachment to key social democratic values (Taylor-Gooby, 1985, 1991).

However, this is not to suggest that ideology was somehow unimportant. It was important, only not in the way that Hall and Jacques and their followers (including Fairclough) suggested. For the processes of ideological struggle on the left, which were to disorientate and immobilize the forces which might have given expression to the more progressive values predominating in British society, were perhaps more important to the successes of the right than any straightforward assertion of their

---

[7]In *Language and Power*, Fairclough (1989) acknowledged the following: "The view of Thatcherism I shall present owes most [in fact almost everything, CC/PEJ] to the political analyses associated with the Communist Party journal *Marxism Today*" (p. 176).

own ideological precepts. Some on the left, not least a certain tendency in the Communist Party of Great Britain represented by Hall and Jacques, were radically undermining the left's remaining, and indeed still very substantial, bases of power. Some, it must be imagined, did this knowingly; others perhaps "ran headlong to their chains," although others still, like some of the skeptics in Glasgow, embattled and disorientated in what were difficult circumstances, were carried along reluctantly, but were unsure about what else to do in the face of "new realities."

The actual trajectory of this tendency is perfectly encapsulated in the fate of the Communist Party under its control. In the early 1970s, this party provided much of the intellectual and moral leadership for the movement that defeated Heath's neo-liberal agenda (Foster & Woolfson, 1986). But now this "old left" was marginalized and expelled, and the organization and its journal were used, with significant effect, to project the ideology, not of the new right, but of the "new realities" and the "new times," which rendered the "old left" with their old "concentrations of power" increasingly obsolete, and demanded "new politics." As this became, as Webster (1984) put it, the "new orthodoxy," the journal was wound up, and the organization itself liquidated.

Yet, for all its claims to be "critical"—revealing connections that would otherwise remain hidden—CDA knows nothing, or at least reveals nothing, of this. Perhaps more strangely, it continues to persevere with the "critical" and "emancipatory" agenda it imbibed from a tendency which has long since abandoned it; almost as if that tendency's trajectory were somehow irrelevant to CDA's own. And herein lies the irony. Fairclough, in more recent work, sets CDA the task of critically challenging "the new capitalism" and "New Labour" with its aggressive deepening of neo-liberal measures. Along this path, CDA "can make a vital contribution on issues which are vitally important for the future of humankind" (Fairclough, 2001, p. 205; see also Fairclough, 2000; Fairclough, Graham, Lemke, & Wodak, 2004). This is entirely commendable. But then Fairclough seems unaware of, or at least reluctant to reveal, the manifest historical connections between the inspiration CDA takes from *Marxism Today*, with its "new realities," "new times," and "new politics" on the one hand, and the emergence of "new realism," New Labour, and "the new world order" on the other. In scholarship, which makes such ado about its "critical" revelation of hidden connections, this lack of "reflexivity" seems striking, and perhaps particularly striking when the language itself seems to offer such obvious clues.

ACKNOWLEDGMENTS

The authors gratefully acknowledge Tim Holmes's permission to cite his unpublished dissertation (Holmes, 1990). Sincere thanks also go to Duncan Sim for a very helpful discussion regarding the origins of Glasgow's "community ownership" program in the mid-1980s. In neither case, however, should the assistance provided be taken to imply any kind of endorsement of the authors' analysis. Grateful thanks are also due to Michael Huspek, and to John Foster.

REFERENCES

Cable, V. (1975). Glasgow: area of need. In G. Brown (Ed.), *The red paper on Scotland* (pp. 232–246). Edinburgh, Scotland: EUSPB.
Collins, C. (1999). *Language, ideology and social consciousness: Developing a sociohistorical approach.* Aldershot, England: Ashgate.
Collins, C. (2000). Vygotsky on language and social consciousness: Underpinning the use of Voloshinov in the study of popular protest. *Historical Materialism, 7,* 41–69.
Cook, R. (1975). Scotland's housing. In G. Brown (Ed), *The red paper on Scotland* (pp. 334–343). Edinburgh, Scotland: EUSPB.
Fairclough, N. (1989). *Language and power.* London: Longman.
Fairclough, N. (1992). *Discourse and social change.* Oxford, England: Polity Press.
Fairclough, N. (2000). *New Labour, new language?* London: Routledge.
Fairclough, N. (2001). *Language and power* (2nd ed.). London: Longman/Pearson.
Fairclough, N., Graham, P., Lemke, J., & Wodak, R. (2004). Introduction. *Critical Discourse Studies, 1,* 1–7.
Foster, J., & Woolfson, C. (1986). *The politics of the UCS work-in.* London: Lawrence and Wishart.
Fowler, R. (1996). On critical linguistics. In C. R. Caldas Coulthard & M. Coulthard (Eds.), *Texts and practices: Readings in critical discourse analysis* (pp. 3–14). London: Routledge.
Fowler, R., Hodge, B., Kress, G., & Trew, T. (1979). *Language and control.* London: Routledge & Kegan Paul.
Gibb, A. (1989). Policy and politics in Scottish housing since 1945. In R. Rodger (Ed.), *Scottish housing in the twentieth century* (pp. 155–183). London: Leicester University Press.
Grieve, R., Clark, I., Finniston, M., & Karn, V. (1986). *Inquiry into housing in Glasgow.* Glasgow, Scotland: Glasgow District Council.
Hall, S. (1988). *The hard road to renewal: Thatcherism and the crisis of the left.* London: Verso.
Hall, S., & Jacques, M. (1983a). Introduction. In S. Hall & M. Jacques (Eds.), *The politics of Thatcherism* (pp. 9–16). London: Lawrence and Wishart.
Hall, S., & Jacques, M. (1983b). The great moving right show. In S. Hall & M. Jacques (Eds.), *The politics of Thatcherism* (pp. 19–39). London: Lawrence and Wishart.
Hall, S., & Jacques, M. (Eds.). (1983c). *The politics of Thatcherism.* London: Lawrence and Wishart.
Hall, S., & Jacques, M. (Eds.). (1989). *New times: The changing face of politics in the 1990s.* London: Lawrence and Wishart.
Holmes, T. (1990). *Local authority stock transfer to community ownership: A study into the policy and practice of government and Glasgow District Council.* Dissertation submitted for the postgraduate diploma in Housing Administration, University of Stirling, Scotland, Department of Sociology and Social Policy.
Ilyenkov, I. (1982). *The dialectics of the abstract and concrete in Marx's capital.* Moscow: Progress Publishers.
Jones, P. (2001). The ideal in cultural–historical activity theory. In S. Chaiklin (Ed.), *The theory and practice of cultural–historical activity theory* (pp. 283–315). Aarhus, Denmark: Aarhus University Press.
Jones, P. E. (2004). Discourse and the materialist conception of history: Critical comments on critical discourse analysis. *Historical Materialism, 12,* 97–125.
Keating, M. (1985, December 20). Community-owned housing in Glasgow facing "suffocation." *Municipal Journal,* 2058–2059.

Kemp, P. (1992). Housing. In D. Marsh & R. Rhodes (Eds.), *Implementing Thatcherite policies: Audit of an era* (pp. 65–80). Buckingham, England: Open University Press.

Kirkwood, C. (1975). Community democracy. In G. Brown (Ed), *The red paper on Scotland* (pp. 85–97). Edinburgh, Scotland: EUSPB.

Malpass, P. (Ed.). (1986). *The housing crisis*. London: Croom Helm.

Matheson, M. (1976). *Housing associations in Glasgow. Discussion papers in planning* (Discussion Paper No. 8). Glasgow, Scotland: University of Glasgow, Department of Town and Regional Planning.

Murie, A. (1996). Housing tenure and housing policy. In H. Currie & A. Murie (Eds.), *Housing in Scotland* (pp. 57–75). Coventry, England: Chartered Institute of Housing.

O'Carroll, A. (1996). Historical perspectives on tenure development in two Scottish cities. In H. Currie & A. Murie (Eds.), *Housing in Scotland* (pp. 16–30). Coventry, England: Chartered Institute of Housing..

Sawchuk, P., Duarte, N., & Elhamoumi, M. (2006). *Critical perspectives on activity: Explorations across education, work and everyday life*. New York: Cambridge University Press.

Sim, D. (2004) Introduction. In D. Sim (Ed.), *Housing and public policy in post-devolution Scotland* (pp. 1–15). Coventry, England: Chartered Institute of Housing.

Stetsenko, A., & Arievitch, I. M. (2004a). The self in cultural–historical activity theory. *Theory and Psychology, 14,* 475–503.

Stetsenko, A., & Arievitch, I.M. (2004b). Vygotskian collaborative project of social transformation: History, politics and practice in knowledge construction. *International Journal of Critical Psychology, 12,* 58–80.

Taylor-Gooby, P. (1985). *Public opinion, ideology and state welfare*. London: Routledge & Kegan Paul.

Taylor-Gooby, P. (1991) Attachment to the welfare state. In R. Jowell, L. Brook, & B. Taylor (Eds.), *British social attitudes: The 8th report* (pp. 23–42). Aldershot, England: Dartmouth.

Toolan, M. (1996). *Total speech*. Durham, NC: Duke University Press.

Webster, D. (1984). *The socialist case for community ownership* (Briefing Paper). Glasgow, Scotland: Glasgow District Council, Housing Department.

Discourses of Labor Protest

Charles Woolfson
University of Latvia, Riga, Latvia
and
School of Law, University of Glasgow, Scotland

This article explores the emergent discourses of labor protest which have accompanied the transition process from communism to the market economy. Building on the groundbreaking theoretical paradigm of V.N. Vološinov and contemporary attempts by Marxist scholars to develop a materialist sociolinguistics, the gradual emergence of class-based labor discourses in the new market economies of Central and Eastern Europe is examined. A number of recent labor protests in ex-soviet Lithuania are examined. The complex articulation of labor identities is charted. Their legitimization, as social actors with "independent" demands, in the context of transitional Lithuanian society, is analyzed through the discourses of protest. Discourses of labor protest have emerged in contestation and tension with seemingly contradictory attempts to impose a "supraclass" ideology. The imposition of both neo-liberal ideology which seeks to exclude organized labor from an independent role in civil society, and at the same time, the cultivation of the language of social partnership, which seeks to incorporate labor in national tripartite structures, are complementary attempts to forestall the emergence of more radical class-based discourses. The emergence of dialogic discourses between labor and capital, and the forms of their social resonance, reveal much about the current limits of labor protest in the new market economies. Such discourses also reveal much about possible future forms of labor contestation, as the new market economies of Central and Eastern Europe are incorporated into the newly enlarged European Union.

This article explores the emergent discourses of labor protest which have accompanied the transition process from socialism to the market economies. It is a first preliminary attempt, based on admittedly fragmentary samples of discourse, to provide a basis for future more extensive analysis. Even these limited snatches of discourse, however, provide a condensed telegraphy of protest revealing the po-

---

Correspondence should be addressed to Charles Woolfson, School of Law, University of Glasgow, Glasgow, G12 8QQ, UK. E-mail: c.woolfson@law.gla.ac.uk

tential emergence of more challenging "emancipatory" discourses (Huspek, 1991). The discourses are comprised of spoken utterances of participants in labor protests captured in news reports, slogans on banners and placards, protest manifestos, and declarations. These are "dialogic" statements of discontent "from below," addressed to ruling authorities and posing uncomfortable, even potentially incompatible questions about the new social order of postcommunism. Very often such dialog takes a moralistic accusatory tone, addressing issues of fairness in society, more particularly of the perceived betrayal of expectations and promises of what a "free," democratic, postsoviet Lithuania would offer to its citizens. Theoretically, this article draws on the work of V. N. Voloshinov, a scholar who laid the basis for a Marxist school of social dialogics during the first phase of socialist transformation in Russia, and whose important theoretical work has been in English translation for some three decades, and although increasingly recognized, hitherto, largely unapplied empirically (Voloshinov, 1973; Woolfson, 1976, 1977). The approach sketched by Voloshinov has however been developed in the active critique of both structuralist and Habermasian approaches to social discourse analysis (Brandist, 2000; Collins, 1999; Foster & Woolfson, 1999; Gardiner, 1992; Jones, 2004; McNally, 2001; Welty, 1989). In contrast to structuralist analyses, priority is given to the linguistic sign in the realized and contested spoken utterance as the vehicle of ideological social consciousness. In distinction, although not necessarily in opposition to, the insights of cognitive cultural theory (Ignatow, 2004), the analysis presented here remains on the terrain of the collective group identities, formed in specific social and historical circumstances. The dialogic realization of utterances is seen as contingent on the underlying and unfolding processes of the new forms of labor's collective alienation in the sphere of production, the systemic relocation of labor within emergent capitalist relations of production. Empirically, postcommunist transition society offers a unique window into these changing forms of consciousness in a changed world, one in which labor's alienation is taking radically new appearances.

Within this altered world, the specific refraction of reality which each ideological sphere attains through the semiotic materiality of signs, achieves particular clarity in the dialogic discourses of labor protest. Vološinov (1973, p. 15) put it as follows: "Every ideological refraction of existence in the process of generation, no matter what the nature of its significant material, is accompanied by ideological refraction in word as an obligatory concomitant phenomenon."

However, in this process, language is no mere mechanistic reflection of the struggle of base within superstructures. Vološinov identified not simply the reflection of reality in signs, but its ideologized refraction, infusing an "inner dialectical quality" in word meaning (Vološinov, 1973, p. 23). This dialectical tension creates a clash of "differently oriented social accents" within one and the same sign community (Vološinov, 1973, p. 41). The refraction of class struggle is registered in what Vološinov (1973, p. 23) termed the "social multiaccentuality" of the ideological sign, in which theme and form of sign are inextricably interconnected and ultimately determined by these sets of contested forces:

> Indeed, the economic conditions that inaugurate a new element of reality into the social purview, that make it socially meaningful and "interesting," are exactly the same conditions that create the forms of ideological communication (the cognitive, the artistic, the religious, and so on), which in turn shape the forms of semiotic expression. (Vološinov, 1973, pp. 22–23)

For these purposes, the "new element of reality" is the complex unfolding of class identities in the newly emergent market economies of postcommunism. This process is conditioned by the legacies and inhibitions of the previous era, but it is also sensitive to the impacts of economic and political change of unprecedented scope and rapidity, no less than the establishment of the new order of the market economy. Dialogic discourse allows us to begin to analyze these impacts within changing forms of social consciousness. Vološinov (1973) suggested the following:

> The word is the most sensitive index of social changes, and what is more, of changes still in the process of growth, still without definitive shape and not as yet accommodated into already regularized and fully defined ideological systems. The word has the capacity to register all the transitory, delicate, momentary phases of social change. (p. 23)

But the "indexical" potential of words, in providing a window into changing social consciousness, is conditioned by contemporary ideological interventions which are themselves politically and socially "motivated" by the need to secure the hegemony of new market forces. Over the period of more than a decade and a half since the collapse of the Soviet Union, an attempt has been made to impose forms of social dialog based on nonclass "shared" assumptions of "social partnership" between labor and capital, "united" in the common project of transition. This has been an acutely "necessary" form of intervention, given the fraught social tensions created by the spiraling inequalities of postcommunist society, and the supplanting of collectivist outlooks and supports with those based on forms of radical individualism. Like all ruling classes, the new elites of postcommunism have attempted to give a supraclass, or eternal and "immutable" quality, to word meaning in language, and therefore, to perceived reality. Above all, it has been necessary to forestall any return to previous "alternative" discourses of socialism, creating a radical rupture in social consciousness, by superimposing a new unified national identity to carry through the awkward business of postcommunist transition. The search for new unifying ideology was well articulated by one spokesperson for the nascent Lithuanian independence movement of the early 1990s: "It is necessary for us to become citizens of Lithuania. It would be our common joy... we would have common duties and common concerns" (Juozaitis, 1990).

Crucial to the consolidation of this constructed unified national identity of "common duties" and "common concerns," was the resurrection or reinvention of symbols of nationhood. This required the negotiation of an uncomfortable authoritarian (largely proto-fascist) legacy from the interwar era of Lithuanian national independence. The resurrection of Lithuanian national identity also entailed the contemporary reinstatement of the primacy of the Lithuanian language over Russian, now the rejected language of the Soviet "occupier," although still the first language of a significant minority, especially of the working population. Largely deprived of the legitimizing resources of past history, and consumed with the expurgation of its more contemporary Soviet history, the nascent independence movement in Lithuania resorted to the creation of a sometimes spurious vocabulary of symbolic unity. Such conscious deployments of meanings and language, however, are always liable to contestation, creating what Vološinov (1973, p. 24) called "dialectical flux" within language. It is this continuing semiotic flux, which potentially poses socially disruptive challenges to the increasingly fragile assumptions underlying the new social order, that is examined here. It is the privileged site within which a more or less fierce and ongoing "socially interested" interrogation of signs between labor and capital takes place.

The study of contemporary labor protests accompanying the class reformation of Lithuanian society provides an empirical field for the application of these theoretical insights, and in the real world, for a contest around the newly constructed "unity" of the Lithuanian nation. The analysis this article seeks to develop is predicated therefore on understanding the actively embodied language of labor protest as the preeminent arena of contested dialogic utterances, viewed in the developing context of rising class tensions. The approach is concrete and historical, and is applied to a specific body of empirical circumstances. Following a brief political and economic analysis of postcommunist Lithuania, its emergent discourses of labor protest accompanying "new elements of reality" in postcommunist labor relations are then examined.

LITHUANIA: UNITY AND DEMOCRACY IN A POSTCOMMUNIST SOCIETY

In the Central and Eastern Europe of the late 20th and early 21st centuries, a double transformation has occurred, first from planned socialist economies to the free market, and from protective economic integration into a politico-economic bloc, to sudden exposure to the raw forces of globalization. In the most recent period, a third transformation has been inaugurated, the wider integration of major parts of the former communist world of Central and Eastern Europe into the European Union project of eastwards enlargement. The massive economic changes that have taken place in Central and Eastern Europe since the early 1990s have been well rehearsed many times. These have included the dissolution of state enterprises, emergent foreign and joint ownership patterns, as well as the massive growth of domestic small and medium entrepreneurial concerns. The transition process to market economies has been accompanied by privatization, bankruptcies, restructuring, the growth of unemployment, underemployment, and a radical "flexiblization" of the workforce (Rainnie, Smith, & Swain, 2002). All of these factors have created a sharp imbalance in power between employers and employees at the workplace and the marginalization of labor rights.

Typical here is the ex-Soviet republic of Lithuania, a small Baltic nation close to Scandinavia with a population of some 3½ million (Woolfson & Beck, 2002). Although one of the smallest countries in the Soviet Union, Lithuania played a pivotal role in its final breakup. Most memorably on August 23, 1989, the formation of a 370-mile human chain stretching from Lithuania in the south, through Latvia to Estonia in the north, linked anywhere from 1 to 3 million "Balts" in a unified popular protest against Soviet rule. The demonstration climaxed a series of denunciations of Soviet occupation, marking the 50th anniversary of the Nazi-Soviet Non-Aggression (Molotov-Ribbentrop) pact, the "secret protocols" of which assigned the Baltic States to the Soviet sphere of influence. These actions, meant to highlight the "illegitimate" character of Soviet rule, symbolized a newly-found Baltic unity and a common striving to "restore" their independence. The Lithuanian Reform Movement (the *Sajūdis* movement for *perestroika*), under its astute leader Vytautas Landsbergis, sustained the ongoing struggle for national independence through the continued mobilization of anti-Soviet sentiment (Lane, 2002). The declaration of the *Sajūdis* showed their close sensitivity to the power of language in political struggle:

> Today all the people of Lithuania know that there is a word in the Lithuanian language which is pronounced with hope. The word is *Sajūdis* (movement). For the first time, the word attained new meaning in the Great Hall of the Lithuanian Academy of Sciences in the late evening of June 3, 1989. Later the word became known to everybody and it came to mean what we call "The Lithuanian Reform Movement." (Lituanus, 1990)

Landsbergis, throughout his long political career thereafter, retained an almost paranoid hatred of all the symbolic manifestations of socialism, the Soviet regime, and its "totalitarian" symbols which he equated with those of Nazi Germany. Lithuania's own complicity in the Holocaust, however, has remained a largely unopened historical chapter. Ninety-four percent of its 240,000 Jewish inhabitants were exterminated, but, until 2006, without a single successful subsequent war crimes trial. To this day, the word "genocide" is almost exclusively linked in Lithuanian political discourse to the repressive actions of the Soviet authorities in the post-WWII period. It is given physical embodiment in the Museum of Genocide located in the former KGB headquarters in the capital city, devoted to the preservation of documents "about the forms of physical and spiritual genocide against the Lithuanian people, the ways and extent of resistance against the Soviet regime" (Lithuanian Museum of Genocide, n.d.).

Although *Sajūdis* won parliamentary elections in 1990, its continuing reliance on the mobilization of symbolic anti-Soviet sentiment was insufficient to sustain its electoral base (Lane, 2002, p. 141). Divisions within its own ranks over major issues like de-collectivization of farmlands alienated key sections of its rural support. By 1992, in the face of sharply deteriorating economic conditions, growing unemployment and hyperinflation reaching 1,000% per annum, the urban working class electorate also rejected the *Sajūdis*.

In what appeared a surprising result, the electorate voted the tried and tested leadership of the now reformed communists of the Lithuanian Democratic Labor Party (LDDP) into office on a program promising greater social protection against the shocks of transition. However, such protective assurances could not be realized within the policy constraints imposed by international financial institutions, and in turn, they too were to lose popular support and power. Moreover, in this unstable political process, the notion of "democracy" as such, was increasingly discredited as a result of its perceived association with gross abuses accompanying the restructuring process of the economy. The rejection of the LDDP was the result of "widespread belief in the corruption of its leading politicians, and the cynical way in which it feathered the nests of the old communist *nomenklatura* at a time when standards of living for ordinary people were in rapid decline" (Lane, 2002, p. 134). In 1996, elections resulted in the formation of a coalition government led by the right-wing Homeland Union (TS) party, a successor to the *Sajūdis* movement. Since then, various coalitions of right-wing parties led by Conservative and Liberal parties, and of centrist parties led by the Social Democratic Labor Party (now Social Democratic Party), have held power in Lithuania although with increasing popular alienation from the political process as corruption and insider-dealing have continued apace.

At the same time, the deep-seated degree of disenchantment with the political process in the new "democracy" continues to be a major issue as corruption and gain-seeking by the new elites erode whatever little legitimacy the new system might have attained. So much so that it has required the importation of a Lithuanian émigré, Valdas Adamkus, to act as a unifying presidential figurehead in an attempt to restore the moral authority of the state. One contemporary observer put it as follows, aptly capturing the linguistic "flux" of the word "democracy" in the context of postcommunist Lithuania:

> The political class mouthed the vocabulary of democracy but sometimes their actions showed either that they did not understand the meaning of the term, or cynically ignored it. The election of President Adamkus in 1997, in a sense an outsider who had spent most of his adult life in the United States, epitomized the contrast between two

political cultures, each using the same vocabulary but differing radically in their understanding of the words. (Lane, 2002, p. 131)

Significantly, Adamkus, politically on the right of the political spectrum, embarked on his presidential electoral campaign by offering himself as the embodiment of nonparty unity under the supraclass slogan, "Accord of the Nation."

PRIVATIZATION AND FOREIGN INVESTMENT

After a hesitant start in restructuring the state-controlled economy, from the mid-1990s onward, Lithuania attempted to consolidate its shift to a market economy by competing aggressively with its neighbors for Foreign Direct Investment (FDI). Lithuanian governments of differing political persuasions sought to attract foreign investors, partly on account of the country's willing, educated, and compliant workforce. According to the Organisation for Economic Co-operation and Development (OECD), the share of FDI in the gross fixed capital formation in the Lithuanian economy increased considerably from 1995, highlighting the increasing significance of FDI in the lucrative privatized sectors. By 1998, FDI net inflows as a percentage of gross domestic product (GDP) were 10.6% for Estonia, 3.5% for Latvia, and 8.6% for Lithuania. This can be compared to 0.4% for Russia and 4.5% for Poland, traditionally the favored site for foreign investment in Central and Eastern Europe (OECD, 2000, p. 12). Cumulative FDI in Lithuania rose from 8 million USD in 1991 to 2,307 million USD in the third quarter of 1999 (Republic of Lithuania, 1999). Outranked only by Estonia as a site for foreign investment, Lithuania maintained a leading position in FDI in terms of dollars per capita among the 13 countries of Eastern Europe for most of the 1990s.

The favorable environment of Lithuania as a site for incoming FDI was highlighted in a report issued by the U.S. Embassy in Vilnius which commented that "most US businesses in Lithuania rate the business environment as among the best to be found in the countries of the former Soviet Union" (U.S. Embassy, 1998). This viewpoint was underscored by Lithuania's labour costs which are "among the lowest in the European Union" (Lithuanian Development Agency, 2004). At the date of enlargement on May 1, 2004, the minimum monthly salary was $176, while the minimum hourly salary was 1 dollar. Foreign multinationals which have invested in Lithuania include Motorola, Mars, Siemens, Telia/Sonera, Philips, Statoil, Shell, Kraft Food International, Philip Morris, SEB, Carlsberg, and Toleram. In terms of industrial sectors, the largest share of FDI is accounted for by manufacturing, which comprises 31.81%, followed by wholesale and retail trade and repair services at 24.53%, telecommunications at 17.94%, and financial services at 13.65% (U.S. Embassy, 1998, p. 20). Survey evidence suggests that this investment position has been attributable to the country's enthusiastic adoption of a business-friendly neo-liberal approach. Thus, an analysis of investment conditions in 27 postcommunist countries, conducted by the *Wall Street Journal Europe* in 2000, ranked Lithuania seventh in terms of governmental efforts to create a favorable climate for foreign investors (Valonis, 2001, p. 34). About two thirds of Lithuania's FDI was accounted for by only five countries, of which the two most important were Denmark (18.2%) and Sweden (17.5%). This was followed by the United States (13.4%), Finland (10.6%), and Germany (7.7%) (OECD, 2000, p. 17). OECD analysts have suggested that "the moderate wage costs and skilled workforce, together with growing market potential, geographic location and economic and political stability," created particular incentives for FDI in Lithuania (OECD, 2000, p. 9). Today Lithuania seeks to entice potential investors with so-called "Free Economic Zones" which offer a string of tax breaks, such as exemptions from corporation tax for 5 years for investments worth over 1 million Euros, customs exemptions, road, property, and VAT (Value Added Tax) exemptions.

The political and business elites have embraced neo-liberal ideology fostering the myth of a stable prospering Lithuania, with few social and economic problems. The January 2001 edition of *EuroBusiness* contained a special Baltic states supplement entitled "New Breeds of Tiger." Among the specific virtues of Baltic Lithuania, *EuroBusiness* noted "aggressive economic liberalization, privatizations, wily courtship of foreign capital and the painful reorientation of trade away from volatile Russia" (p. 69). All of these factors were said to "have underpinned a truly remarkable flourishing of prospects, generating year on year of high yet sustainable growth" (*EuroBusiness*, 2001, p.69). The report went on to record that, according to *The Wall Street Journal*, Lithuania, and its next door neighbor Latvia, superseded only by Estonia, outranked Denmark, Finland, and Germany in the "league table of economic freedom" (*EuroBusiness*, 2001, p. 70). The reality of the privatization of the Lithuanian economy and the drive for foreign investment has been rather less unproblematic. The early 1990s, in particular, were marked by severe economic difficulties in the aftermath of independence with the collapse of the Soviet planned economy, although GDP grew strongly thereafter, before declining again in 1999 in the wake of the Russian financial crisis of August 1998. At that time, Russia was Lithuania's leading trading partner and still remains important today.

The form of privatization itself did much to undermine the attempt to establish a supraclass "unity" of Lithuanian society. The rapid expropriation of state assets in the process of transition to capitalism was effected, in the main, via emerging business criminality. Privatization, the economic engine of the transition process, according to its most enthusiastic proponents, was supposed to make workers "co-owners," and fulfill egalitarian "social justice" and equity objectives (Lithuanian Free Market Institute, 2000). Yet within a matter of a few years, sometimes even within months, the majority of privatization vouchers handed out to workers in former state enterprises were sold on the black market for cash. They ended up in the pockets of enterprise managers on extremely favorable discounted terms, jarring with "public expectations…strengthened by propaganda, promising high dividend rates, high profitability of the shares and higher living standards" (Maldeikis, 1996, p.

3). So great was public disaffection and unrest concerning "corruption and the influence of organized criminal groups" over the process of privatization that it was temporarily halted (Maldeikis, 1996, p. 16). The distribution of assets before auctions, via "payments to organized criminal groups for the right to acquire particular assets, the selling of 'insider' information by officials and their participation in privatization process" produced a negative popular view of the whole process of privatization, akin perhaps to a sense of collective victimization (Maldeikis, 1996, p. 16).

This appraisal is no mere academic commentary. As Minister of Economics, Maldeikis later resigned from a Conservative-led coalition government over shady privatization deals. This government was itself eventually to fall in October 1999, over the controversial sale of a strategic oil refinery in Northern Lithuania, Mazieukiu Nafta to Williams International, a U.S. energy company. Williams obtained the Mazieukiu Nafta complex for what appeared to be a bargain basement price, acquiring 33% of the stock (hence the operational control), for a mere $150 million. In so doing, it also succeeded in imposing a coercive condition on the Lithuanian Government in the form of an obligation to provide matching investment in the complex to the tune of $350 million. This was a burden which the then faltering Lithuanian economy could hardly carry (*The Baltic Review*, 2002). The subsequent disappearance and assassination of the local manager of the Williams, together with his son, added to the swirl of dark speculation. Williams International, for its part, was later to gain minor notoriety in the United States for involvement in the "gouging" of de-regulated energy resources which led to statewide electricity blackouts across California. In its Lithuanian operation, Williams failed to deliver its expected share of the promised investment to modernize the Mazieukiu facility. Before it departed from Lithuania, the company compounded its "treachery" by the sale in 2002 of its controlling assets to the Russian-owned Yukos oil company.

The more recent history of Lithuanian political life has been scarred by continuing allegations of the involvement of organized crime at the highest levels of the state, adding to the popular disenchantment with many of the earlier myths of a united nation struggling to find its place in a new world. The political corruption of the privatization process has continued. In 2004, the elected president of Lithuania, Rolandas Paksas, was formally impeached, the first European head of state to be so removed from office, for alleged links to Russian organized crime groups and interference in the privatization of remaining state assets by his advisors. Among the most prominent of these was an international arms dealer accused of selling helicopter spare parts to the arms-embargoed government of Sudan.

The darker side of the transition process has also been evident in the sheer scale of impact of economic reforms on the workforce. The first decade and a half of transition was marked by a massive deterioration in the wages and working conditions of labor, and the growth of high levels of unemployment. However, mass hardship was not simply a passing feature of the early turbulent years of transition. In 2 years, between 1997 and 1999, as a result of ongoing privatizations in Vilnius, the capital city of Lithuania, nearly one quarter of job positions disappeared in the largest five factories. In the Kaunas industrial region, where the biggest number of factories are located, the number of jobs in large enterprises decreased by about 40% (United Nations, 1999, p. 64). According to one analysis, these job losses have disproportionately affected older workers, the unskilled, and women, whose participation declined from 56% to 50% (Dovydenienė, 1999). The process of a marginalization of a large group of workers has been accompanied, as elsewhere in Eastern Europe, by a sharp growth in income differentials. In 2000, one third of families with three or more children, representing 16% of the population, were estimated to live below the official poverty line of 50% of the average wage (Republic of Lithuania, 2000). Conservative estimates of Lithuania's "informal" economy suggest that this sector employs some 300,000 workers, or more than 20% of the total working population (Bagdzevičenė & Belazrienė, 2001, pp. 25–28). All of these workers, by definition, are excluded from protection with regard to secure and safe employment conditions.

In sum, since its exit from the Soviet sphere of influence, Lithuania's path of transition to the market economy has been guided by an aggressive neo-liberal program. Despite local disputes over the pace and nature of privatization, this project has been largely uncontested among the political classes. Pressures, in particular from the International Monetary Fund and the European Bank for Reconstruction and Development, have left successive governments little room for maneuver. Although increasingly viewed with suspicion and disillusionment at a mass level, 80% of enterprises were rapidly privatized. Today, only a few significant enterprises remain in state control.

LABOR INCORPORATION AND LABOR PROTEST

The levers of economic and political power, both at national level and in the workplace, have been firmly gripped by the new employer class. So far, however, organized trade union resistance has failed to emerge in the forms that are commonly understood in Western democracies. The classical labor dispute has been a rarity in Lithuania, especially in recent years. When it has occurred, it has experienced significant legal as well as organizational impediments. The U.S. Embassy report on Lithuania that was discussed earlier noted reassuringly that "labor unions are relatively uninfluential" and that the country "has not seen any major industrial strikes since regaining independence" (U.S. Embassy, 1998). In fact, in 1992, public sector workers took industrial action, as well as hairdressers, photo studio operators, and transport drivers. However, the Country Studies/Area Handbook Series sponsored by the U.S. Department of the Army noted that "strikes and other confrontations between labor and management … are limited by the nascent free-enterprise system and the perception that employment alternatives are limited" (U.S. Department of the Army, n.d.). Systematic collection of statistical data about the strikes in Lithuania only started in the year 2000. According to these statistics, in the year

2000, there were 56 strikes (including 21 warning strikes), and during 2001, there were 34 strikes (including 29 warning strikes). Most of these strikes were organized in educational institutions of the state sector, although there were also strikes in transport and manufacturing sectors. The main reasons for striking were conflicts concerning late or nonpayment of wages (European Foundation for the Improvement of Living and Working Conditions, 2002). In the more recent period, the ever-watchful U.S. Department of State has observed the continuing absence of strikes. In its *Country Reports on Human Rights Practices* (2003), it noted that, according to the Lithuanian Department of Statistics, no official strikes were registered that year. Farmers protesting low milk prices blocked roads and as a result, "criminal proceedings were initiated" (U. S. State Department, 2003). There were also "a number of unregistered protest actions by the employees over wage arrears and dismissals" (U.S. State Department, 2003). The lack of registered strikes does not mean that labor conflicts have been entirely extinguished, however. Although major union-led industrial disputes have been the exception, it is precisely these "unregistered protest actions," or embryonic collective actions by labor, which are significant indicators of continuing underlying and often suppressed forms of conflict. It is just such protest actions which comprise the main body of material analyzed here.

For the new elites of postcommunism, any collective assertion of labor rights and identities, outside of strictly bounded limits, has been viewed as a potential impediment to their economic survival. In essence, free market philosophy has remained largely uncontested by any significant countermovement in the first phase of transition. Yet the transition process has been accompanied by a sharp polarization of society, as previously described, in terms of the growth of inequality. With this has come the emergence of the objective basis for class-based discourses of labor protest. However, the articulation of such discourses has been far from straightforward. A legacy of anti-Sovietism has meant that any collective class-based expressions of discontent, for example, through the organized trade union movement, have been largely discredited. The former pro-Soviet Communist Party was banned from 1991. Its ailing first secretary, Mikolas Burokevicius, languished in prison a decade later for involvement in the half-hearted and ill-founded attempt to reassert Soviet authority during a brief but bloody intervention by Soviet armed forces in 1991. Meanwhile, the "reformed communists" of the independence movement have merged almost seamlessly into interlinked social democratic political and trade union formations.

In the emerging pro-independence movement in Lithuania in the late 1980s and early 1990s, unlike the campaign for independence in neighboring Poland, there was no involvement of collective labor through industrial actions such as strikes. This was probably because of the integration of the Lithuanian trade unions in the all-Soviet trade union structures of the USSR, and the significant ethnic Russian component of the Lithuanian industrial working class which was somewhat ambivalent about the burgeoning independence movement. Indeed, a sporadic although largely unsuccessful attempt was made to organize factory strikes against the *Sajūdis* by the pro-Moscow anti-independence *Yedinstvo* (Unified) movement, especially in the later phases of the independence campaign. In general, however, the Russian-speaking section of the working class remained essentially a passive spectator throughout these protracted struggles.

Thereafter, the formerly unified Soviet-led all-union trade union confederation divided into four separate federations aligned with various political groupings across the politically tolerated spectrum, from centrist Social Democratic to rightist Christian Democratic (Dovydenienė, 2000). The official trade union center was renamed after independence, as the Confederation of Free Lithuanian Trade Unions (CFTU). At that time, in the early 1990s, it claimed a membership of 1.1 million. In 1993, the CFTU joined eight other unions that also had been part of the All-Union Central Council to form the Lithuanian Trade Union Centre (LTUC). The Lithuanian Workers' Union (LWU) was formed in 1990 as an alternative to the CFTU. Unlike the CFTU/LTUC, the LWU was an early supporter of Lithuanian independence from the Soviet Union and actively sought Western trade union contacts. Over the following decade and a half, the various trade union confederations fought among themselves for control over an ever diminishing number of registered members and the assets of the former Soviet trade unions. In 2003, the unions were collectively stripped of these assets, thus further severely restricting their ability to act.

At a mass level, the trade unions, hitherto at least, have not been "trusted" institutions of the "reconstituted civil society," primarily through their association with the previous system. Thus, trade union membership in Lithuania, as elsewhere in Central and Eastern Europe, has plunged to catastrophically low levels in recent years and is currently about 14% of the workforce, mainly concentrated in the public sector, with collective bargaining agreement coverage being even lower (EIROnline, 2005). Moreover, a particularly restrictive set of antistrike laws is in place with an extensive list of "essential services" in which the right to strike is either removed or severely limited (Woolfson & Beck, 2003). With elaborate mandatory prestrike procedures for conciliation, and a threshold requirement of at least a two-thirds majority of workers voting in favor of industrial action, these make the pursuit of collective industrial protest very difficult, and indeed are the cause of continuing concern by international human rights bodies (Office of the United Nations High Commissioner for Human Rights, 2004). Thus, in the first phase of transition, legitimized oppositional collective discourses have struggled to emerge in any defined class sense. As such, the fragmentary discourses of labor protest chart the difficult road that Lithuanian labor has traveled in the last decade and a half.

Paradoxically, in the early years of transition, organized labor in the trade unions retained a "voice" in policy discourses at the national level. In the attempt to guarantee "social peace" and "labor quiescence" in the process of transition to the market economy, various forums of tripartite "social dialog" were introduced at national level from the early 1990s onward throughout Central and Eastern Europe. Such tripartite forums were created largely on the advice of international agencies such as the International Labour Organization (ILO), seeking to promote "social partnership." Thus the new Lithuanian Labor Code of 2002 specified collective labor relations as an expression of "social partnership." Under Article 39, "Reconciliation of Interests of Labor Relations Subjects," it was deemed that "in order to actualize social partnership, this Code and other laws shall establish that social partnership may be realized by way of bargaining and agreements" (Republic of Lithuania, 2002, Article 39). Thereafter, no less than six articles of the Code spell out the forms of such social partnership arrangements in detail. Such social partnership arrangements differ from the state-sponsored participation of trade unions in national policy arenas under the previous regime. For over a decade, these forums have provided an arena of "regulated discourse" and a strictly bounded legitimacy to an otherwise discredited trade union movement. This type of "social dialog" promoted shared assumptions, albeit sometimes reluctantly embraced, of the necessity of "joint sacrifice" in carrying through painful economic restructuring. The attendant ideology of "social partnership" served not only to confirm a rather spurious equality of interlocutors, but also an equally spurious notion of "equality of burden-sharing" between labor and capital which was promoted on the basis of a common national identity in the postcommunist period (Ost, 2000). In fact, the so-called "peak organizations" of labor had only the most shaky constituencies to provide them with legitimacy in their self-appointed role as representative voices and guarantors of "social peace."

Although such social dialog "captured" national trade union leaderships and provided them with much needed legitimacy and purpose in the postcommunist setup, tensions began to emerge. In formal political discourse, a debate ensued between the more radical proponents of unrestrained free market and neo-liberal paths to transition, and those who sought a more gradual path of transition to the market. The latter proposed more measured and socially inclusive approaches to transition based on social democratic assumptions, increasingly based on the European Union's "social model" to which these states now sought accession. These emphasized notions of social cohesion and integration, seeking to preserve a "social dimension" within the harsher context of market reforms. Yet, although at the national level the appearance of a broad consensus was maintained, at the enterprise and workplace level a new dynamic was beginning to assert itself, as workers responded to the imposition of a significantly more stringent labor regime than anything previously experienced under the former system. This new labor discipline was typically summed up in the following ironic observation: "At least under Communism we only had to work eight hours a day. Now we have to work all the hours of the day."

Some measure of the increasingly desperate condition that labor found itself in can be gauged from the following incident. In its review for the year 2000, Lithuanian state television included brief news footage of a distraught middle-aged man being wrestled to the ground by three police officers, before being bundled into the back of a police Lada. The man, who had doused himself in petrol and was about to set himself on fire in front of the presidential palace in the capital city of Vilnius, was shouting "let me die—I have nothing left to lose." In this one single utterance, the despair of the postcommunist dispossessed proletariat is articulated. The incident was a solitary act of desperation by one of several dozens of workers who had been on hunger strike in protest against the nonpayment of wages by defaulting employers of bankrupt enterprises. As it happened, the news clip summed up much about the state of Lithuania's economy and labor relations. The enterprise from which this particular worker had come, Litoda, was located in a town in the west of the country and formerly produced synthetic leather. In the new Lithuania, in which Mafia men and their legions of adolescent imitators strut in regulation black leather, the demand for its synthetic imitation has slumped, although export of this product had proven almost impossible. Hunger strikes by cheated employees lasted for 6 weeks and saw their participants removed to hospitals, with probable permanent physical damage.

This brief and desperate cameo of individualized public protest action is remarkable only in the sense that it was captured on camera. Most such acts of attempted self-destruction are entirely "voiceless" and take place in private hidden corners. Lithuania currently has the highest official rate of suicide in Europe, and possibly in the world (Mite, 2002). Moreover, these rates have been rising in recent years since the mid-1990s. In 2001, the Department of Statistics recorded that 1,533 Lithuanians committed suicide, something like 4% of deaths overall, or 44 deaths per 100,000 of population (compared to U.S. and Europe rates of about 11 per 100,000; Republic of Lithuania, 2001). This rate is more than twice the average for the candidate countries and more than four times the average for the European Union (EU; WHO, 2001, 2002). The extraordinarily high overall rates of suicide are mirrored in another remarkable phenomenon, the numbers of employees who kill themselves in the workplace. Recorded workplace suicides more than doubled from 14 (for the years 1995 to 1997) to 37 (for the years 1998 to 2000; State Labor Inspectorate via V. Michalkeviciate, personal communication, October 8, 2001). The National Health Council Report for 2000 commented that "suicides at work may be linked with work strain, inability to adjust…to new, more complex working conditions, delayed payment, threat of unemployment, (abusive) behavior of employers or authorized persons" (National Health Council Annual Report, 2000). Although it is impossible to gauge how many of the total of suicides are the result of work-related stress or other psychological pressures of occupational origin, it would seem that the new workplace environment of postcommunism plays a significant role.

LABOR MARKET LIBERALIZATION

A second contemporary labor protest in Lithuania, although it was not yet a full collective withdrawal of labor based on specific workplace demands, reveals a shift from largely individualized forms of protest. If anything, however, it was a substitute symbolical protest performed on behalf of workers by their organized leadership and was an expression of tensions previously unarticulated within the national social dialog arrangements. After a period of left-led government in the earlier part of the 1990s, a Conservative government took power in Lithuania in the late 1990s. This Conservative government was routed at the polls in October 2000, in the backwash of renewed disillusion with privatization and falling living standards. In the run up to the election, bitter public controversy over the sale of one third of the state-owned Mazieukiu Nafta oil refinery to the U.S. Williams oil company had the seemingly perverse effect of restoring some of Lithuania's national pride in the achievements of Soviet-built industry (Blocker, 1999; Pasukeviciute & Roe, 2001). However, the election did not see the Left regain power, although the Social Democrats won the largest number of seats in the *Seimas* (parliament). Instead, a coalition of liberals and the New Union (social liberals) assumed office with a radical program of antilabor, "business-friendly" proposals.

Within weeks of gaining office, the new government published a resolution spelling out its intentions (*Seimas* of the Republic of Lithuania, 2000). Under the heading of "Liberalization of Labor Relations," this resolution proposed a number of changes to trade union and employment laws which were to become part of the new government's action plan of the first 100 days. These included the following:

1. An approved typical form of an employment contract to be recommended but not compulsory.
2. All restrictions in concluding any type of civil contracts between natural persons as well as between natural and legal persons to be lifted.
3. Restrictions on temporary employment contracts to be gradually phased out.
4. Statutory requirements for an employer to inform the social insurance commission (Sodra) on the employment of a person on the same day and dismissal from employment within three working days to be no longer applicable.
5. Mandatory working time records no longer to be kept.
6. Requirement that employees have employment identification documents to be waived.
7. Compensation for public servants and other employees as provided by existing legislation to be reduced in amount.
8. Employers no longer required to consult trade unions before making workers redundant, where the worker is a member of a trade union.
9. If there is an interruption to production and the employer wishes to temporarily redeploy a worker but the employee refuses to accept redeployment, the employer obliged to pay only one third of the minimum wage rate instead of the full statutory minimum rate.
10. Workers who receive training at employer's expense to compensate the employer if changing employment.

The proposed measures, officially aimed at "reducing unemployment in Lithuania," were part of a concerted attempt to create labor market "flexibility" which appeared as a major threat to existing trade unions. Indeed, following the publication of these proposals, the four trade union confederations, united for the first time since independence, threatened nationwide industrial action. Articles on employee rights and conditions appearing in the Lithuanian press exposed "routine slavery" conditions (Žiūkienė-Lavaste, 2002). By the early Spring of 2001, the trade union opposition at the national tripartite level led to a postponement of the planned liberalization package. On March 23rd, nonetheless, the *Seimas* (parliament) passed new liberalization legislation that amended *inter alia*, the *Law on Employment Contracts*, the *Law on Wages*, the *Law on Holidays*, and the *Law on Trade Unions*. The typical labor contract was duly abolished, with a new noncompulsory "sample" labor contract being included as an Appendix of the *Law on Employment Contracts*.

In response to these proposed measures, labor protests took place outside the homes of Liberal and New Union Members of Parliament (MPs), whereas over a hundred trade unionists from throughout Lithuania attended as "silent witness" at the plenary debate on the new legislation in the *Seimas*. Opposition Social Democratic coalition MPs, who had sponsored the trade unions' "silent witness" in parliament, called on the President not to ratify the new law. Presidential ratification, however, duly followed, with trade union representatives "threatening" to boycott future social dialog discussions, on the grounds that no prior discussion of these crucial measures had taken place in the Tripartite Council. During this dispute, overt protest on the part of the trade unions created public relations risks for them. Protest action was directed against individual MPs who supported the liberalization measures. In most instances, these protests involved small quiet pickets of perhaps a dozen or so smartly dressed men and women, standing with placards in dignified order outside the homes of MPs. Some newspapers claimed the protesters had caused a fatal heart attack to the mother of one MP and denounced the intimidation of families and innocent children. On TV, the wife of one MP was seen on the television news arriving in a Mitsubishi four-wheel drive vehicle, unmolested by the "pickets." The direct "personalization" of the protest against the liberalization measures was easily construed by a hostile media as "intimidatory." The linguistic "flux" of social opinion, to return to Vološinov's perspectives, was captured in television broadcasts. These broadcasts provided pictures, remarkable in the context of media representations of postcommunist society, of the condensed and semantically loaded telegraphy of protest. One placard read almost cozily, only to end with stinging rebuke: "Dear Neighbors — We elected your neighbor Rolanda Pavilionis but he voted in the *Seimas* for measures that will make you a slave without rights." On other placards there was an even more bald accusatory tone: "We did not elect you to vote for our enslavement," and, "We did not elect you to vote to remove our rights and jobs." One protest placard displayed a message asking the following of a member of parliament: "Do you know what an autocracy at work means G. Dalinkevicius?" Another banner contained a cartoon representation in one corner of a boss aggressively pointing a finger at the figure before him of a worker on his knees. The personalization of "you" in the slogans implied a real human identity as its referent. The "you" is named, it is someone known to and present in the community, albeit that he or she is a member of Parliament. Such key words as *autocracy* (*savivalė*) and *slave* (*vergas*) may seem quaint to outsiders, but they are imbued with accusatory, potentially explosive, meaning. Lithuania was meant to have emerged democratically reborn, but now the forces of the free market seemed to undermine that common interest. It is perhaps not going too far to suggest that the use of these terms was an implicit riposte to the language of the post-1991 order, in terms of its self-justification as one of "freedom," and in contrast to the "autocracy" of the previous order. The "one-nation" ideology which was an important political lever in the dislocation of Soviet power, now had ironic resonance in the post-Soviet period. In the new democracy, where politicians are supposed to represent the "unified" interests of the people, the sense of betrayal, was palpably conveyed by such personalized admonishments.

The *Panorama* evening news review program on Lithuania's national television Channel 1 (March, 23, 2001), invited viewers to e-mail the station's Web site with their opinion of the consequences of the liberalization law in response to four assertions that had all been aired by various spokespersons in the "debate" on liberalization earlier in the broadcast. These were as follows:

1. Social and economic rights will be reduced.
2. The power of employers will be increased.
3. There will be a decrease in trade union members.
4. The business environment will be improved.

The Minister of Labor and Social Affairs, Vilija Blinkevicuite, reassured viewers that "Lithuania will abide by the European Charter on social rights and will guarantee these rights whatever the government" (LTV, *Panorama* Channel 1, March 23, 2001, author's recording). At the same time, the chairman of the parliamentary Committee for Labor and Social Affairs commented as follows: "We cut compensation for dismissal by three times...if employers have to pay out 20,000 Litas (£3,500) for each dismissal, companies go bankrupt" (LTV, *Panorama* Channel 1, March 23, 2001, author's recording). In an attempt to claim the moral high ground, the Social Democratic trade union federation took out a full-page advertisement in the daily press, headed as follows: "Warning to Lithuanian Members of Parliament and the electors," explaining the basis of their opposition to the new measures. The names of those 40, mainly Social Democrat MPs, who voted against liberalization, were listed above those of the 50 or so Liberal and New Liberals who voted for the legislation (Respublika, 2001). Speaking for the trade unions, the prominent trade unionist and Social Democrat MP, Roma Dovydeniene, spelled out the following opposing view: "trade union power will be reduced and the number of trade unions will decline. Employers do not want trade unions inside their companies. If the employer wants, the worker can now be easily dismissed" (LTV, *Panorama*, March 23, 2001, author's recording). Given the magnitude of the threat posed to basic labor rights by the new liberalization legislation, it can be argued that the trade unions acted with "restraint." Most likely, this restraint was a mark of their overall weakness, and perhaps, a recognition that, in Lithuania, concerted worker protests could not yet be fully legitimized. On a more positive note, the scale of the assault on labor rights provoked united trade union opposition for the first time since independence, and in 2002, the two major trade union centers amalgamated into one body.

"MUTED" COLLECTIVIST DISCOURSE: POLICE OFFICER INDUSTRIAL PROTEST

In this section, "muted" collectivist discourse is analyzed. It concerns a group of workers not normally associated with public protest actions: the police. The Constitution of the Republic of Lithuania and the 1991 Law on Trade Unions recognize the right of workers and employees to form and join trade unions (Republic of Lithuania, 1991a). Article 1 of the Law on Trade Unions extends this right to employees of the police and the armed forces via statutes regulating their activities. In the case of police officers, this is the Law on Police (Republic of Lithuania, 1991b). Article 8 of this law allows for the "Realization of Professional Interests" and states that "Police officers may establish societies, clubs, professional unions, and other associations in order to meet their professional, cultural, and social needs" (Republic of Lithuania, 1991b, Article 8). However, the Law on the Regulation of Collective Disputes of 1992 does not allow withdrawal of labor by employees involved in law enforcement and state security:

> It shall be prohibited to call a strike within the structures of internal affairs, national defense and national security... The demands of the employees of such services ...shall be considered by the Government of the Republic of Lithuania. (Republic of Lithuania, 1992, Article 10)

This prohibition on the right to strike has had particular effects on the police as an occupational group in Lithuania. In the early period of independence, there were few attempts to raise their status and effectiveness as professional law enforcement officers. The origins of labor unrest among this sector date back to 1997, when government promises of higher wages for senior officers were not matched by an appropriate budgetary allocation. As a result, funds that were initially earmarked for lower ranking police officers were diverted. Rank and file police complained of low wages, as well as lack of funds for basic equipment, including replacement uniforms and petrol for vehicles (at that time more than half being Soviet-built Ladas with a tendency to self-immolate, and no match for the new

BMW-driving criminal classes). Police in the capital city were on occasion without facilities for long-distance telephone connections, due to unpaid bills, whereas some 6,000 employees had been laid off. It was against this background of rising frustration that the police officers' trade union, the Union of Police Constables and Police Employees, was established.

By December 2000, the police trade union was sufficiently well organized in the Vilnius region to mount a public protest. This consisted of a "lunchtime walk through Gedimino Prospect," the main thoroughfare of the capital, by around 400 policemen and women in full uniform supported by firebrigade colleagues. The "walk" culminated in the handing over of a petition listing their grievances to the *Seimas* (*Lietuvos Rytas*, 2002). The leader of the police trade union commented as follows: "We have no money for lunch, so at least we will have some fresh air to breath." A simultaneous demonstration was held in Klaipėda, a port city in northern Lithuania. Two further mass demonstrations of this nature were held (June 2001 and May 2003), involving police trade unionists from the increasingly well-organized outlying regions of Lithuania, as well as at least one spontaneous sit-in at the end of shift over delayed payment of wages, a fairly remarkable occurrence in view of the strict police discipline code. In the case of the mass demonstrations, the Lithuanian police trade unionists were latterly able to call on the support of Italian and German police union colleagues who marched side by side with the Lithuanians as fellow members of the European Police Trade Union Confederation, CESP. This is the first recorded example of international trade union solidarity at the European level in a dispute involving a section of the Lithuanian workforce.

Senior police officers who had been publicly hostile to the first protest action, verbally at least, supported the demands of their lower ranking officers. A measure perhaps of their growing strength as a union, was the absence of reported victimization of activists, commonplace in Lithuanian labor relations. The police trade union now claims to have recruited about 1,000 of the capital's 2,500 police and some 5,000 out of the 11,000 for the whole of Lithuania (Interview, 2004). If correct, these figures represent the highest trade union density of any sector of the workforce. The public impact of these demonstrations, especially of the first, was sufficiently great to produce a substantial new budgetary allocation. It also brought to a halt the ongoing redundancies of police officers. Nevertheless, some important grievances have remained unresolved and the language of incorporation has only partially met its goal of dampening labor protest among Lithuanian police.

The promised increase in salaries for lower ranking police has not yet emerged. Moreover, a new statute governing police work stipulates shift work in excess of the 48-hr allowable maximum working week according to ILO's Convention. This adversely affects more than half of police officers who work in shifts and has resulted in a formal complaint to the ILO Committee of Experts on the Application of Conventions and Recommendations, to which the government of Lithuania has been invited to respond (ILO, 2004). Besides unwelcome exposure to international scrutiny with respect to labor standards in Lithuania, the police trade unionists' protests have a singular significance, in that nationwide collective labor protest appears to be emerging, even in sectors of the workforce that are legally precluded from taking part in collective withdrawal of labor. Meanwhile, in an extraordinary Congress of Lithuanian Trade Union Confederation, the former Chairperson of the Lithuanian Trade Union of Constables and Police Employees, Artūras Černiauskas, was elected as a new Chairperson of Lithuanian Trade Union Confederation (LPSK), perhaps the first of a new generation of more combative labor leaders to emerge in postcommunist Lithuania.

The response of the Lithuanian authorities to labor unrest among the police has been predictable, the incorporation of the new police trade union into a framework of social dialog and the recognition of the union as a "social partner." Yet how far this "incorporation" represents an enduring "restabilization" is a more open issue as the conclusion section suggests. Police officers in their thousands subsequently undertook legal action against the state to recover lost wages, although so far the promised threat of (illegal) strike action has not yet materialized.

EUROPEAN PROTEST

One of the most important inhibitions on the growth of organized labor in postindependence Lithuania has been sustained anti-union harassment. In Lithuania today, in common with many other new democracies in Central and Eastern Europe, there is widespread ongoing victimization and intimidation of trade union activists. The International Helsinki Federation for Human Rights (2003) country analysis for Lithuania has noted the following:

> In 2003 a new Code on Civil Procedure will come into force, which, in specifying that trade union lawyers are no longer allowed to represent and defend their union members on appeal to the Supreme Court, effectively violates provisions of the European Social Charter. In 2002 Lithuanian law guaranteed certain rights for Lithuanian workers, however the practical and economic mechanisms necessary for the effective protection of these rights were not established.... Lithuanian employers were effectively able to dictate working conditions. Employers worded employment contracts with terms favorable to them, leaving the worker with no employment guarantees.

In a further report, the Helsinki Committee on Economic, Social and Cultural Rights (2004) noted under "Labor Rights" in Lithuania, that "The authorities continued to tolerate gross violations of employees' rights: individuals were illegally fired after fictitious liquidation claims and rehired as new workers with fewer rights" (p. 274).

Following privatization of the railroads, anti-union activities on the part of management were experienced by members of the Lithuanian Railway Workers' Trade

Union. The Deputy Chairperson of the union was dismissed three times, although on each occasion ordered to be reinstated following a court ruling. However, no sanctions were imposed on the managers concerned. A locomotive-driver who had given 25 years of satisfactory service, was dismissed after taking an active role in the union. At the end of 2004, the driver was in the process of appealing in the courts against unfair dismissal, although as indicated, without the possibility of representation by a trade union lawyer (International Confederation of Free Trade Unions, 2004a, 2004b). In only a few cases, however, has employment reinstatement followed a ruling of unfair dismissal by the courts. To draw attention to these and other abuses, the Railway Workers Union decided to take their grievances to Brussels, on the very eve of Lithuania becoming a full member of the European Union. Accordingly, in late March 2004, two Lithuanian railway trade-unionists began a pavement hunger strike opposite the entry to a European Commission building, near the Schuman metro station in Brussels. Their sleeping bags and umbrellas were framed by a placard which announced the following in English: "Lithuanian hired workers' hunger action." Before starting the hunger strike, the union had sent a "petition" to the president of the European Parliament, to the then European Commission Chairman, and to the European Commissioner responsible for EU enlargement. In this communication, the trade unionists drew attention to the "horrible situation of hired workers and cynical violation of independent organizations' labor rights, and pitiable social security in candidate countries." The commencement of the hunger strike was accompanied by a declaration in which the new point of reference of labor injustices in Lithuania was clearly identified. Union chairperson, Vladimiras Troschchenka (Socialist Party of Lithuania, 2004), put it as follows:

> Although politicians of Lithuania and other countries joining the EU fulfill all the requirements of European Union Commissioners, the EU Parliament and the Commission are *straightforwardly responsible for the situation of hired citizens in our states, which today is tragic.*

The declaration continued with a seemingly reasonable, but politically "impossible," demand—that Lithuania should conform to EU labor standards, or its membership should be renegotiated:

> Breach of labor rights of hired workers and their organisations is an everyday reality in the candidate-states, and nobody is going to solve that. Therefore we request that the enrolment of the new States in the European Union be suspended and new talks on the enrolment's conditions take place. During the talks, there should be a discussion and adjustment of the protection of labor rights and social environment to present EU-standards, orders and terms.

The other Brussels hunger-striker was Leonidas Malomuzhas, the dismissed locomotive-driver referred to earlier, who at this point had already experienced seven months without salary. Malomuzhas's comments were aimed at the "citizens of Europe":

> It is not important for me if I go to hunger strike, either in my homeland Lithuania, or here, in the capital of Europe. The difference is that here I can *draw the attention of Europe's citizens to the appalling situation* in the labor market of the Candidate States. (Socialist Party of Lithuania, 2004; emphasis added)

Within a week, after a period of "administrative custody" during which they were fingerprinted, the two Lithuanian trade unionists were summarily deported in handcuffs from Belgium. Accompanied by a three-car, high-speed police escort, with full sirens blaring, both the protesters were bundled onto a plane to Lithuania without explanation, or a reasonable opportunity to seek legal assistance. Troshchenka put it as follows: "Workers fighting for their rights have been treated as gangsters! This is the reality of European Union" (Socialist Party of Lithuania, 2004). The next day, a declaration detailed at length their summary treatment and harassment at the hands of the Belgian authorities. Their disturbing account of these events asked the following: "Is the Convention on Europe's human rights and main freedoms valid in Brussels [also] for East Europe's inhabitants?" (Troschchenka, 2004).

COLLECTIVE LABOR DISCOURSE IN THE ENLARED EUROPEAN UNION

The question that remains is whether the emerging discourses of protest may be assuming more clearly defined oppositional collective class-based articulation, more in keeping with commonly understood expressions of labor protest in established Western democracies. On May 1, 2004, Lithuania, together with seven other Central and East European states, joined into the enlarged European Union. The choice of "Labor Day" as the date of accession of the former communist states was an inspired act of bare-faced symbolic theft. However, it may yet come back to haunt the masters of the new Europe. With entry into the European Union, latent dissatisfaction with the consequences of the pursuit of neo-liberal economic policy among the workers in postcommunist countries such as Lithuania, may acquire a new dynamism. The European social model is meant to balance the market and social priorities. European Union Directives address many aspects of working environment, including health and safety conditions, hours of work, consultation and information rights, and so forth, whereas the accompanying European Charter of Fundamental Rights legitimates the basic right to collective forms of protection through trade unions, up to and including, the right to strike. Thus with European accession, a new assertive impetus may be given to the discourses of collective labor rights, resonating with underlying accumulated grievances of the workforces. Whether such impetus will be realized depends, to some extent, on the trade unions' organizational capacities, which as noted, are currently seriously depleted.

Until now, the discourses of labor discontent in postcommunist Lithuania have mainly expressed themselves through individual and symbolic acts of resistance. In part, the lack of strike action is also the result of two generations in which there would have been little collective labor action, and possibly a decline of class consciousness. In part also, the undeveloped nature of this discourse is the result of the breakup of any collective class confidence—and of the explicit ideological marginalization and suppression of the language of class action, through concepts of "common interests" and institutional structures of "social partnership." Emergent labor protests, therefore, have taken both a personalized and a political form—rather than immediate resort to the use of "traditional" collective strike action. Protests have included hunger strikes and public demonstrations by placard-bearing "victims" of injustice. These have occurred outside the employer factory gate or residence, as well as outside the symbolic site of the State, be it the presidential palace and parliamentary building, or the offices of the European superstate. Occasionally, and most dramatically, protest actions have assumed huge personal sacrifices, setting up the dialogic tension of accusatory symbolic gestures which have resulted in real harm to those making them.

The future may be rather different. Following the expansion of class horizons accompanying accession to the wider enlarged European Union, the potential for larger-scale, more organized strikes in postcommunist societies can now be recognized. Given the predominantly neo-liberal approach of ruling elites in the new EU member postcommunist states, as their one-sidedly class-based nature becomes increasingly transparent, the legitimizing potential of demands for labor rights may reinfuse the trade union movement with combative vigor. With that, the temporary national unity of the early postcommunist years may finally be dissipated. The first significant blows in the coming battles have already been struck, in terms of an employers' offensive, through the imposition of labor market liberalization measures in new labor codes throughout Central and Eastern Europe. The reactions of labor can only grow more defined, especially as the established European trade unions extend their solidarity actions to the new member states. In addition, paradoxically, the accession to the EU of former communist countries now brings the uncomfortable requirement for the relegalization of Communist Parties. The prospects for mass influence of Marxist ideas in Eastern Europe are uneven at this time. Nevertheless, the class-fracturing of the language of "social partnership" has begun. The failures of European social democracy to protect workers' rights may in the future become subject to renewed critique and development in a more explicitly class-based direction.

Thus, it can be argued that there will be an inevitable shift from more individualized and muted acts of protest to more open collective forms of labor struggle as the process of European integration proceeds, and as links between organized workers are solidified and capacities strengthened on a pan-European basis. Respondents in national polls were asked whether in the coming year, "strikes and industrial disputes in this country will increase, decrease, or remain the same?" France topped this list, with 60% expecting more strikes and industrial disputes, followed by Ecuador (59%), the Philippines (58%), and in fourth place, Lithuania (55%). Next on the list was Poland (53%) and Romania (51%), ranking three European postcommunist states among the top six countries (Roy Morgan Research Centre, 2000). A recent analysis of industrial relations in four Central and East European countries also warned that it is "not clear yet whether the fairly peaceful character of industrial relations in Central and Eastern Europe can be maintained in the future" (Toth & Neumann, 2003). Again, the conclusions of this survey could equally well apply to Lithuania. The study noted that "unavoidable major reforms in the public services are still to be carried out in all of the countries considered" (Toth & Neumann, 2003). Such reforms, it added, "might lead to the further radicalization of public service trade unions," an area in which trade unions are actively recruiting (Toth & Neumann, 2003). Equally, the four-country survey noted the possible emergence of "a more aggressive trade union strategy in the post-enlargement phase, which would seek the redistribution of the benefits of productivity gains in the context of employees' expectations related to accession to the EU" (Toth & Neumann, 2003).

The accession of Lithuania, along with seven other Central and East European countries to the enlarged European Union, may mark a turning point in the dynamics of labor protest. Its accompanying discourses, although not in any sense determinative, may undergo significant change. The compass of ideological reference is pointing away from the past negative associations toward trade unions and collectivism in which the Soviet system is now a fading memory of a decade and a half ago. A new reference point is emerging, where trade unions are increasingly to be seen as necessary active defenders of legitimate labor rights, in the face of continuing employer abuse. Moreover, the right to the collective withdrawal of labor, and to free association and collective bargaining, are both endorsed as democratic rights at European and international levels in conventions to which Lithuania is a signatory. This new reference point provides a discourse of democratic rights legitimizing independent collective trade union action, up to and including, the right to strike. A free society is, by definition, a society of "free" collective bargaining. It suggests that the (re)legitimization of collectivist labor discourses may be one of the most significant, although unintended, consequences of the eastward expansion of the European Union. The gathering prospect of an end to postcommunist "labor quiescence" brings with it potentially incompatible challenges to the current order of neo-liberal economic prescriptions, a development which, in itself, seems likely to be increasingly reflected in the discourses of labor protest.

ACKNOWLEDGMENTS

John Foster and Chik Collins provided valuable comments on earlier drafts of this article. All errors and omissions remain the responsibility of the author.

REFERENCES

Bagdzevičienė, R., & Belazrienė, G. (2001). Shadow economy in Lithuania. *Lithuanian Business Review, 8*, 25–28.
Blocker, J. (1999, October 21). (RFE/RL) Weekly Reports, Lithuania: Crisis Reflects New Eastern Skepticism. Retrieved April 8, 2006, from http://www.rferl.org/features/1999/10/f.ru.991021140250.asp
Brandist, C. (2000). Bakhtin, Marxism and Russian populism. In C. Brandist & G. Tihanov (Eds.), *Materializing Bakhtin: The Bakhtin Circle and social theory* (pp. 70–93). London: Macmillan.
Collins, C. (1999). *Language, ideology and social consciousness—Developing a sociohistorical approach.* Aldershot, England: Ashgate.
Declaration of Lithuanian railway trade-unions' chairman Vladimir Troshchenka. (2004). Is convention on Europe's human rights and main freedoms valid in Brussels for East Europe's inhabitants? April 2, Vilnius (author's possession).
Dovydenienė, R. (2000). *Trade union responses to globalization in Lithuania.* Geneva: International Labour Organisation, Institute for Labour Studies, Labour and Society Programme. Retrieved April 8, 2006, from http://www.ilo.org/public/english/bureau/inst/download/dp11199.pdf
EIROnline. (2005). Lithuania—Trade unions in focus. Retrieved April 8, 2006, from http://www.eiro.eurofound.ie/2004/12/feature/lt0412102f.html
European Foundation for the Improvement of Living and Working Conditions. (2002). *Social dialogue and conflict resolution in Lithuania.* Retrieved April 8, 2006, from http://www.eurofound.eu.int/publications/files/EF0451EN.pdf
Foster, J., & Woolfson, C. (1999). How workers on the Clyde gained the capacity for class struggle: The Upper Clyde Shipbuilders' Work-In, 1971–2. In J. McIlroy, N. Fishman, & A. B. Campbell. (Eds.), *British Trade Unions and Industrial Politics, Volume 2, The High Tide of Trade Unionism, 1964–79.* (pp. 297–325). Aldershot, England: Ashgate.
Gardiner, M. (1992). *The dialogics of critique.* London: Routledge.
Huspek, M. (1991). Language and power. *Language and Society, 20*, 131–137.
Ignatow, G. (2004). Speaking together, thinking together? Exploring metaphor and cognition in a shipyard union dispute. *Sociological Forum, 19*, 405–433.
International Confederation of Free Trade Unions. (2004a). *Annual Survey 2004 Violations of Trade Union Rights.* Retrieved April 8, 2006, from http://www.icftu.org/survey2004.asp?language=EN
International Confederation of Free Trade Unions. (2004b). Europe: Alarming trend in anti-union measures in Eastern Europe. Retrieved April 8, 2006, from http://www.icftu.org/displaydocument.asp?Index=991219351&language=EN
International Helsinki Federation for Human Rights. (2003). *Human rights in the OSCE region: Europe, Central Asia and North America, Report 2003 (Events of 2002), Lithuania Report, June 24.* Retrieved April 8, 2006, from http://www.ihf-hr.org/documents/doc_summary.php?sec_id=3&d_id=3938
International Labor Office. (2004). Letter from Director of International Labor Standards Department, to Lithuanian Trade Union of Constables and Police Employees (received January 16) (authors' possession).
Interview by C. Woolfson with Arturas Navaitas, head of the Union of Police Constables and Police Employees, Vilnius, February 4, 2004.
Jones, P. (2004). Discourse and the materialist conception of history: Critical comments on critical discourse analysis. *Historical Materialism, 12*, 97–125.

Juozaitis, A. (1990) Statement of member of the Sajūdis initiative group [Electronic version]. *Lituanus, Lithuanian Quarterly Journal of Arts and Sciences, 36,*1.
Lane, T. (2002). *Lithuania stepping westward.* London: Routledge.
Lietuvos Rytas. (2002, December 16). *Dignified walk of police,* p. 2.
Lithuanian Development Agency. (2003). *Advantage Lithuania.* Retrieved April 8, 2006, from http://www3.jetro.go.jp/iv/j/fdi/step02/seminar/pdf/040218lithuania.pdf
Lithuanian Free Market Institute. (2000). *Privatization in Lithuania, analysis.* Retrieved April 8, 2006, from http://www.freema.org/Research/Privatisation.phtml
Lithuanian Museum of Genocide, Homepage. (n.d.). Retrieved April 8, 2006, from http://www.genocid.lt/Muziejus/eng/muzeum.htm
LSDPS 'Profesinis solidarumas'. (2001, March 22). *Respublika,* p. 6.
Maldeikis, E. (1996) *Privatisation in Lithuania: Expectations, process, consequences.* Retrieved April 8, 2006, from http://www.som.hw.ac.uk/cert/wpa/1996/dp9603.pdf
McNally, D. (2001). *Bodies of meaning: Studies on language, labor and liberation.* Albany: State University of New York Press.
Mite, V. (2002). Baltics: Suicide rates in transition states among world's highest. Retrieved April 8, 2006, from http://www.rferl.org/nca/features/2002/04/09042002073543.asp
National Health Council. (2000). *Occupational health and safety at work* (Annual Report 2000, Part 4.10). Vilnius, Lithuania: Occupational Medicine Center.
OECD. (2000, July). Foreign Direct Investment Impact and Policy Analysis—Lithuania (OECD Working Papers, VIII, No 92). Paris: Author.
Office of the United Nations High Commissioner for Human Rights (2004). *Concluding observations of the Committee on Economic, Social and Cultural Rights: Lithuania.* 07/06/2004. E/C. 12/1/Add.96. Geneva, Switzerland: Author. Retrieved 8 April 2006, from http://www.unhchr.ch/tbs/doc.nsf/(Symbol)/E.C.12.1.Add.96.En?Opendocument
Ost, D. (2000). Illusory corporatism: Tripartism in the service of neoliberalism. *Politics and Society, 28,* 503–530.
Pasukeviciutë, I., & Roe, M. (2001). The politics of oil in Lithuania: Strategies after transition. *Energy Policy, 29,* 383–397.
Rainnie, A., Smith, A., & Swain, A. (Eds.). (2002). *Work, employment and transition: Restructuring livelihoods in post-communism.* London: Routledge.
Republic of Lithuania. (1991a). On Trade Unions, Article 3. Freedom of Activities of Trade Unions. Article 4, The Legal Basis of Trade Unions, Law No. I-2019, November 21.
Republic of Lithuania. (1991b). On Police, Article 8. Realization of Professional Interests, Law No. 1–851, December 11.
Republic of Lithuania. (1992). On the Regulation of Collective Disputes, Law No. 12386, March 17.
Republic of Lithuania, Department of Statistics. (2000). *Statistical Yearbook of Lithuania 2000.* Vilnius, Lithuania: Author.
Republic of Lithuania, Department of Statistics. (2001). *Mirties priezastys 1999–2000—Causes of Death* (Report No. A302). Vilnius, Lithuania: Author.
Republic of Lithuania. (2002). Labour Code Part II, Collective Labour Relations Chapter VII, General Provisions, Articles 40–47.
Republic of Lithuania. (2003). On internal services, Law No 1X-1538, May 1.
Roy Morgan Research Centre. (2000). *Polls.* Retrieved April 8, 2006, from http://oldwww.roymorgan.com/polls/2000/3270/page-3.html
Seimas of the Republic of Lithuania. (2000). *Resolution on the Program of the Government of the Republic of Lithuania for 2000–2004.* Vilnius, Lithuania: Republic of Lithuania.
Special Report, Baltic States. (2001, January). *EuroBusiness Magazine, 2*(8), 69–98.
Toth, A., & Neumann, L. (2003). *Labour dispute settlement in four central and eastern European countries.* Retrieved April 8, 2006, from http://www.eiro.eurofound.eu.int/2003/01/study/index.html

United Nations. (1999). *United Nations Lithuanian Human Development Report, 1999.* Vilnius, Lithuania: UNDP.

U.S. Department of the Army (n.d.). *Country Studies/Area Handbook Series, Lithuania.* Retrieved April 8, 2006, from http://countrystudies.us/lithuania/17.htm

U.S. Embassy. (1998). *Country commercial guide: Lithuania.* Vilnius, Lithuania: Author.

U.S. State Department. (2003). *Country reports on human rights practices 2003.* Retrieved April 8, 2006, from http://www.state.gov/g/drl/rls/hrrpt/2003/27850.htm

Valionis, A. (2001). Investment yields returns. *Lithuania in the World, 9,* 4.

Vološinov, V. N. (1973). *Marxism and the philosophy of language.* New York: Seminar Press.

Welty, G. (1989, August 17). *A critique of Habermas' proposed reconstruction of historical materialism presented to the Czechoslovak Academy of Sciences.* Retrieved April 8, 2006, from http://www.wright.edu/~gordon.welty/Habermas_89.htm

WHO. (2001, September 12). *Accession — Is it healthy? Health prospects in countries that are candidates for accession to membership of the European Union.* Retrieved April 8, 2006, from http://www.euro.who.int/mediacentre/PressBackgrounders/2001/20010927_5

Woolfson, C. (1976). The semiotics of working-class speech. *Working papers in Cultural Studies 9.* Birmingham, England: University of Birmingham.

Woolfson, C. (1977). Culture, language and the human personality. *Marxism Today, 21,* 229–240.

Woolfson, C., & Beck, M. (2002). Re-mapping labour's rights: The case of transitional Lithuania. *Europe-Asia Studies, 54,* 749–769.

Woolfson, C., & Beck, M. (2003). The right to strike, labor market liberalisation and the new labor code in pre-accession Lithuania. *Review of Central and East European Law, 28,* 77–102.

Žiūkienė-Lavaste, L. (2002, Feburary 23). In the kingdom of women-slavery is routine. Lietuvos Rytas, pp. 1, 8.

On the Philosophical Credentials of the Discourse Society

Darryl Gunson
School of Social Sciences, University of Paisley, Scotland

The work of Jürgen Habermas is both an example of discourse that has provoked oppositional standpoints, as well as at the same time purporting to establish and justify a framework that places discourse at the heart of morality. Morality, that is, with a capital M; morality conceived of in terms of the normativity that is found wherever we can ask what we ought to do. The claim that is embodied in Habermas's Critical Theory is that the contestation of norms in modern societies must be constrained by the demands of reason and its requirement of universalism. This manifests itself as a "Discourse Ethics," which is devoid of any substantive commitment to the "good life" and offers what are the minimal but rationally binding procedural rules that ought to govern the resolution of contested normative claims. In other words, providing certain "ideal standards" are attended to, we should encourage people to talk more when they are in disagreement with others. At one level, this conclusion—we need to talk more—might seem fairly innocuous although superficially appealing to students of language and communication. However, there is more to this framework than the surface banality might suggest and it is my contention that this is best appreciated by considering the more philosophical justifications that Habermas provides. The philosophical context that makes Habermas's work so interesting and relevant, both theoretically and practically, lies in the way Habermas presents the "communicative solution" as being the only way of engaging with and overcoming the philosophical problems that a "discourse of modernity" has revealed.

In the contemporary academic climate it may sound archaic, if not totally redundant, to approach social-theoretic questions[1] from a perspective that places rationality and universality at its center. Indeed, the notion that we should still hold onto this

---

[1]Of course there are many kinds of question that may fall within the disciplinary boundaries of Social Theory, but I have a quite specific kind of question in mind. The questions referred to here concern normative projects rather then descriptive–explanatory accounts of the social world.
Correspondence should be addressed to Darryl Gunson, School of Social Sciences, University of Paisley, High Street, Paisley, Renfrewshire, PA1 2BE, Scotland. E-mail: darryl.gunson@paisley.ac.uk

legacy of the enlightenment is bound to seem naïve in the extreme to some. It may be Foucault's (1967) theses concerning the historical discourses on reason and "unreason" and how madness is, in some sense, a construction of such discourses that makes this standpoint seem outmoded, or it may be his later claims (1977) that technical rationality, exemplified in modern science and technology, is at the service of regimes of discipline and surveillance that is the source of disquiet. Others may have taken Jean-François Lyotard's (1984) distrust of universalist–rationalist philosophy to heart with its rejection of the grand narratives of modernity, whereas others have united under the Derridean "deconstructionist" banner to reject the "logo-centrism" of Western philosophy. Despite this cultural shift, Jürgen Habermas remains the leading advocate of a social philosophy (1984, 1987a) that does have rational-universalist pretensions and he has, over the years, elaborated a detailed account of the role that these concepts and their central role in linguistic communication have in the "project of modernity;" a project that is, he argues, unfinished (1996).[2] Now the twin concepts of rationality and universality, central as they are to Habermas's social theory, actually provide the philosophical grounds for his argument that the progressive ideals of modernity can best be served by a culture where open discourse is the preferred way of settling important normative questions. Indeed, as we shall see, the charge of naivety is attracted not because of Habermas's fondness for discourse, for most social theorists and philosophers see a role for it, but rather for his contention that (oppositional) discourses can be resolved rationally. The general problem here according to critics is that rationality has become suspect, especially when conceived along universalist lines, because it is thought to marginalize the voice of the "other" and consequently runs roughshod over the diverse forms of human thought and practice that our (post) modern situation requires us to appreciate.

Opposed to this suspicion, Habermas's work, controversially, aims to tie social theory to a particular version of the philosophy of language. This "linguistic turn" purports to have several theoretical advantages in this domain, especially when the connection is made with his moral philosophy, what he calls "Discourse Ethics." The basic idea here is that what delimits the realm of morality in modernity can be divined by paying attention to certain norms embedded in the linguistic process of coming to a consensus over what should be done in particular situations where the questions of truth, right or wrong, and sincerity emerge. These rules or norms are the rational scaffolding on which morality rests. It is, however, important to note that Habermas's theory refers to norms at two distinct, but related, levels. The norms that actual communities agree as valid are what we might call those that are

---

[2]As Mitchell Stephens in the L.A. Times Magazine so aptly put it: "A debate has been raging in the world of scholars and intellectuals. On one side are the 'postmodernists'—the thinkers whose ideas inspired the playful, hybrid buildings, outfits and artworks that now grace the American landscape; the thinkers who encouraged a generation of graduate students to 'deconstruct' such long treasured notions as 'reason' and 'justice'. The major figure on the other side of this debate is Jürgen Habermas" (Stephens, 1994, p. 26).

immanent to the process of deciding truth, right from wrong, or establishing what might be the best course of action. Mere agreement, however, is not sufficient to establish such norms as valid. They must be the upshot of a process leading to a rational consensus rather than one that is merely de facto, and therefore there is considerable emphasis by Habermas on the inner logic of moral argumentation. Even at this level of abstraction, we can note the implied connection between normativity, reason, and justice. A rational consensus will be above the influence of subjective power, which tends to distort normativity to fit the interests of the powerful. This thought leads to a consideration of norms that are thought to operate at what we can call the metalevel. These norms are those that form the framework that governs the conduct of discourse. They are the presuppositions of discourse: no one should be excluded; all have the right to have their views heard, and to criticize those of others; only those norms that can be accepted by all as regulating common or general interests are valid. These are those norms that are thought to embody the enlightenment ideals of universalism and rationality and they are thought to yield a framework that is minimal, but rationally binding. It lays no claim to adhere to particular values, but rather outlines a procedure by which norms may be established. It is by considering the process by which norms are generated that the rationality of decisions concerning social ends may be assessed.

The project of modernity has the aim of increasing the scope for rational decision making and in so doing increasing the amount of freedom in our societies. The thought is that rationality can be emancipatory because it is embodied in the basis of our communicative competence and communication is essentially freedom enhancing. Morality[3] and the normativity so essential to modernity is legitimated by being provided with foundations. The foundations are minimal and devoid of content, but they are at the same time procedural and rationally compelling. The content of morality is the upshot of the rational process that Habermas champions, whose foundations have an essential connection with the pragmatics of communication because it is the reconstruction of our basic linguistic competence that is supposed to yield the blueprint of metanorms to guide discourse. It is important to note here that the framework to which I referred earlier is one that can be understood and assessed as a heuristic that presupposes the domain of the moral. It is therefore a prescription as to how moral matters should be rationally settled which might be endorsed or rejected for many different reasons by theorists: for being too complicated, too expensive, or for taking too much time. Put like this, we have two things:[4] first a thesis about the pragmatics of communication and a recommenda-

---

[3] Although not an intuitively comprehensible distinction, it is one that Habermas invokes to demarcate universal normative principles (*Moralitat*) from the particular values that arise in the context of everyday ethical life (*Sittlichkeit*).

[4] It is, I argue, essential to understand that both of these theses are part of the discourse-ethical project, and that one cannot adequately consider the two theses in isolation from each other. Furthermore, we will be able to see more clearly how Habermas intends that "discourse ethics" is not really an optional heuristic, but it is the only rational route available to us.

tion for using certain principles therein as a blueprint for assessing the rationality of decisions for social action, but also, and importantly, there is a thesis regarding the realm of morality itself on whose foundations the first thesis rests.

It is my contention that when seen aright, the idea that discourse or communication is at the heart of a free society, is not just an optional extra, not something that we can choose from a host of alternatives, but something that is inextricably linked to freedom, and something that is, as I said earlier, rationally compelling. However, as already mentioned, this idea has come under attack from some very influential sources and the viability of such a project has been questioned. It is my contention that despite the fashionable—almost *de rigueur* in some circles—distaste for universalism, and the criticisms it attracts, there is still enough in Habermas's project that is viable; enough, that is, to secure the theoretical credentials of the "discourse society" as a blueprint for enlightened societies of the 21st century.

COMMUNICATION, DISCOURSE, AND FREEDOM

The linguistic turn that Habermas's work took during the 1980s was focused on the quite abstract business of drawing out the structure of speakers' linguistic competence. The project (Habermas, 1979, pp. 1–68), subsequently entitled "Universal Pragmatics," was significant in its treatment of language not in terms of syntax, or in terms of its semantics, but in terms of its pragmatic properties. It sought to focus on the things that speakers do when they use language: on speech acts. Insofar as it did this, the overall ambition for the project was that of "reconstructing the validity basis of speech" (Habermas, 1979, p. 4). If the emphasis on speech acts provides the thesis with its pragmatic orientation, then the universal part of the project has to do with the contention that there are basic competencies that are part of one's implicit knowledge—one's know-how—that are genuinely universal. All competent speakers of all languages are, it is argued, possessed of a core of implicit, practical knowledge. This is the foundation for the ability to use language that is routinely displayed in everyday, often mundane situations. This project therefore has a kind of quasi-transcendental character because the task of making the "presuppositions" of linguistic competence explicit is similar in some respects to Kant's transcendental arguments regarding what reality must be like if humans are to have any knowledge of it at all. It is, however, only quasi-transcendental because it contends that its conclusions are not just based on pure aprioristic deduction, but are constrained by empirical observations of actual speech (Habermas, 1979; Wood 1984).

Drawing on a novel mixture of speech-act theory and Kant-influenced Weberian concepts of cultural rationalization and differentiation, Habermas first makes the controversial claim that underlying all potential uses of language is the primary objective of reaching an understanding or consensus. More fully he argues that a number of claims are always implicit whenever we try to communicate with others; a speaker is

1. *Uttering* something understandable.
2. Giving (the hearer) *something* to understand.
3. Making himself *understandable*.
4. Coming to an understanding *with another* person. (Habermas, 1979, p. 2)

So the speaker selects and uses an expression that is, in convention with the dictates of that particular language, comprehensible. In so doing, he or she is also providing the hearer with an object of understanding with the intention of communicating something true, or at least a content that is valid, to share knowledge with the hearer. Intentions, it is suggested, should also be uttered sincerely so that the hearer can believe the speaker. Finally, the utterance that is chosen must be right, or appropriate, in accordance with the normative background that governs linguistic usage. It is on observations such as these that he gives substance to his view that fundamental to all speech is the type of action aimed at *Verstandigung*, reaching understanding. And that goal—the "inherent *telos* of speech"—is to bring about "an agreement…that terminates in the intersubjective mutuality of reciprocal understanding, shared knowledge, mutual trust and shared accord with one another" (Habermas, 1979, p. 2).

These presuppositions of communication are fleshed out even further by the suggestion that communication inevitably involves the raising of certain "validity claims," which correspond to certain "domains of reality." Reciprocal understanding, shared knowledge, mutual trust—consensus—are based on the recognition of the various corresponding validity claims that are routinely raised in communicative contexts. These are as follows: truth, rightness, truthfulness, and comprehensibility (Habermas, 1979). So, on the supposition that the inherent telos of speech is communication—understanding via consensus—and that this is correctly analyzed along the quasi-transcendental lines noted earlier, we have the more detailed analysis of the presuppositions involved whenever communication is the aim of a range of different categories of speech act. The delineation of speech acts correspond to a "Kantian grid" of the "objective world" of external nature, the "intersubjective world" of social norms—morality—and the "inner world" of subjective expression and emotion.

Whenever we use our language with the aim of communicating something, we raise validity claims. Offering anything at all as a possible object of understanding entails an obligation on the part of the speaker to explain what the utterance means if asked. Thus, failure to respond satisfactorily to the question "what do you mean?" invites the charge of irrationality. Such a response will, quite obviously, appeal to the norms and conventions of the particular language and may, often, be redeemed immanently by making them explicit. Habermas's point here is that it is a presupposition of all communication that speakers can, at the very least, come to a consensus about the meanings of words and therefore the meaning of speech acts. Whenever there is disagreement as to meaning, the fact that we are routinely able to communicate anyway suggests that for Habermas, there is a rational pragmatic obligation on the part of coconversationalists to enter into a discourse about the correct meaning of words and expressions, and further, that our competence suggests that rational consensus on such matters is possible.

Moreover, whenever we aim to communicate something of a factual nature about the world, we do, implicitly at the same time, claim to be able to legitimate our assertion. It is part of the structure of the pragmatics of constative speech acts that speakers be able to redeem the implicit claims they entail. So, part of our competency is constituted by the requirement to be able to answer, satisfactorily, according to the appropriate norms, the following question: "How do you know?" or "why should we believe you?" Suitable ways of redeeming validity claims about the objective world might be as follows: "I've seen it with my own eyes" or "I've just read it in a scientific journal," and so on. When the norms appealed to are rejected, or queried, the fact that we are able to communicate and arrive at consensus suggests that speakers are able to enter into a theoretical discourse aimed at resolving differences as to the appropriate norms relating to evidence necessary for redeeming the validity claims of contested constative speech acts. Similarly, normative or regulative speech acts, relating to the "social world," are themselves always resting on implicit validity claims. For any speech act that purports to moral or normative correctness, the utterer is required, as a matter of rationality, to provide grounds for his or her act. To use a simple example, the professor who asks the student to leave her class, is required, so the theory goes, to be able to give an appropriate response if the student requires further justifications. "Why should I leave?" needs to be met by at least indicating the norms that make it appropriate that the professor may, in this context, make such a request. However, just as was the case with constatives, mere identification of the relevant norms may not suffice to ensure the success of the speech act. When a norm is disputed, the supposition is that parties to the dispute are able and rationally required to undertake a discursive examination of the norms in question with a view to coming to a consensus about them.[5] That is, a "practical discourse" is required when the identification of a norm is not sufficient and the supposition is not just that this is rationally required, but also, importantly, that consensus is achievable; that speakers could, if the occasion demanded it, actually come to a consensus over disputed norms.

---

[5]I have referred to the discursive obligations discussed here as having a " 'double normative' context" (Gunson & Collins, 1997, p. 283), but I don't think that is quite right. All the contexts are doubly normative in the sense that rationality requires that one ought to redeem validity claims if required by referring to the conventional norms for doing so (or at least the ones that are being appealed to), and also, where this does not suffice, one is rationally required to enter into discourse about the status of the normative framework that is being appealed to. What is, perhaps, slightly different with respect to "regulatives" is that they are already normative in the sense of aiming at changing peoples' behavior, whereas "constatives" and "representatives" are not.

Finally, with speech acts of the expressive mode referring to "'My' world of internal nature," the implicit claims are not quite those of the previous categories; not so much truth or rightness, not so much an obligation to provide proof, or one to highlight the normative framework being appealed to, but rather one of providing grounds for belief in the truthfulness of the utterer; that is, grounds for the coconversationalist to believe that the speaker is sincere. Such grounds may well be assurances from the speaker, or consistency with past and subsequent behaviour, but the point is, again, that the structure of communication has an implicit normative dimension.

What has all this to do with discourse one might reasonably ask? The connection with the pragmatics of linguistic usage and discourse lies in the nature of validity claim redemption presupposed by linguistic competence. The suggestion is that the empirical fact of our general competence with language presupposes that we are also potentially capable of resolving normativity rationally through discourse; at the heart of our linguistic usage is a communicative rationality. It is through an examination of language—a project of "reconstructive science"—that Habermas hoped to forge the blueprint for a social ethics based on discourse. So what is this Discourse Ethics? The short answer is that Discourse Ethics lays claim to revealing the procedural framework that is necessary for resolving disputes, particularly those with normative implications, in a rational manner. Following Hegel, we might say that the rational society is the moral society, which is at the service of freedom. Increasing freedom[6] is the emancipatory ideal that Habermas takes to be the legacy of the enlightenment.

Developing this thought we may say that a society begins to fulfill its emancipatory potential when the preconditions for rational practical discourses are institutionalized. Such preconditions are, it should be noted, universal. They are meant to be applicable across the board to any society and this is one of the core ideas that have, as we shall see in a moment, attracted the ire of some commentators. Thus, not only is the rational society one that employs instrumental reason in deciding how to achieve social ends, but it also employs communicative reason when those ends themselves, or the general norms that constrain such ends, are contested. Communicative reason is that which is employed in coming to an understanding or consensus and is inherent in communicative competence. In practical discourse, it is claimed that speakers aim to, and consider it possible that they can, achieve a rationally motivated consensus regarding the contested norms. Here it is considered important to distinguish between a de facto consensus and

---

[6]Of course "freedom" itself is a controversial concept, but I cannot go into this matter here except to add that by freedom I do not (just) mean that bulwark of modern liberalism—the negative freedom of Isaiah Berlin—freedom to do just anything without external constraint, but rather I have in mind an account that is, perhaps, more Hegelian. That is, a free society is one that has maximized its own internal self-rule; it provides freedom to pursue the rational course of action, not from an individualistic perspective, but from the perspective of the general good.

one that is genuine or rationally motivated. It is only the latter that has the potential to increase freedom and justice, because it is only a rationally motivated consensus, it is claimed, that can strip away distortions in the discourse that arise from particular strategic interests. The consensus must be at the service of the general interest. Insofar as the practical discourse is in the service of such an interest, it must meet certain requirements, requirements that are already presupposed in everyday communicative contexts. The presuppositions of such competence, taken together, constitute what Habermas called the ideal speech situation.

The ideal speech situation is, as the title suggests, not to be found in actual practical discourses, but is rather a counterfactual presupposition that all speakers cannot but anticipate. Its key element is the absence of all constraints on participants in a practical discourse except those demanded by reason. So participants should be free to employ all communicative speech acts, to raise questions and to provide evidence constrained only by the minimal validity claims associated with communicatives that require that speakers prove to be intelligible. In addition, stemming from the analysis of representatives, it is contended that all participants in a discourse be allowed the opportunity of putting forward their attitudes, feelings, and intentions regarding the issues at stake, thereby going some way to ensuring that the ensuing discourse is free from constraints that may distort the communicative process. The underlying validity claim is, as already noted, that speakers are sincere in their arguments. The corresponding institutional constraints on the discourse must be such that speakers are able to be sincere without the threat of pressures or sanctions either internal or external to the speech situation.

Similarly, all participants in the discourse should be free to use regulative speech acts. That is, they should be free to raise issues, forbid arguments, and question the normative contexts that may militate against the appropriateness of some arguments rather than others. This would go some way to ensuring that norms invoked to block some arguments and allow others to proceed are not one sided, or invoked without scrutiny from the strategic perspective of some of the participants in the process. So, not only does this validity dimension constrain the discourse by requiring that the appropriateness of arguments be agreed on, but it also allows (due to the second normative aspect of regulatives) that participants be able to question those very norms invoked as redemptions as to the appropriateness of specific arguments raised in the debate.

So we have here a model of communication, with its analysis of speech acts and the types of validity claims that may be raised and their modes of redemption from which an ethical theory—Discourse Ethics—is derived. Social justice requires rational norms to serve as guides for action, which are procedurally determined under conditions that approximate to the ideal speech situation. Thus the institutionalization of the conditions for realizing the ideal speech situation becomes one of the central objectives of critical theory. Put like this, the project of critical theory in late modernity becomes one of encouraging, supporting, and persuading that more, not less, open conversation, debate—discourse—is the mark of a rational society. But, importantly, one of the key marks of the rationality in this sense is adherence to the universal principles of discourse ethics.

There are many examples of how this basic framework has been used to illuminate the potential and limits of communication in social action contexts. Here I sketch a few. Certainly one very useful application in the British context has been the attempt to assess the rationality and therefore the justness of policy decisions arising from government-ordered public inquiries (Kemp, 1985). Others have explored the usefulness and the limits of Habermas's framework in understanding the dynamics and the obstacles to the success of government-led urban renewal "partnerships" in the west of Scotland (Gunson & Collins, 1997). Indeed, Habermas (1989) is well known for supporting the idea that the "public sphere" that emerged in Europe, initially among the intelligentsia, might yield valuable insights for contemporary societies as to how an area of public life, where intersubjective agreement on values and standards has been reached to further sociopolitical ends, might exist relatively autonomously of the state. Habermas's studies into this phenomenon are instructive precisely because they indicate the ways that discourse is important to a rational society, but also in that they provide useful clues as to the conditions in which the public sphere becomes less effective. For example, the period where this arena for public discussion and debate was most effective was before its structural transformation in the 18th and 19th centuries. With the onset of industrial capitalism, the public sphere was opened up to more voices, which paradoxically led to a narrowing of the interests effectively expressed. This "privatization of the public sphere," a liberalization of market relations that reduced the autonomy of the public sphere from state interference, actually led to an undermining of the very aspect that had proved to be most effective: its tendency to set aside special interests in the pursuit of the common good. Habermas, of course, argued that an increased inclusiveness ought not to go hand in hand with the narrowing of interests subject to rational public discussion, but for all that it is instructive that the contemporary and historical examples that might approximate to anything resembling Habermas's framework do not, on closer inspection, measure up very well to the ideal. Indeed such a paucity of examples as to how all this could be practiced merely adds to the growing suspicion, noted earlier, that this kind of social theorizing has had its day. Such skepticism is particularly vivid when we begin to make the link between Habermas's technical, philosophical work and that which is closer to sociology and social policy. Although there is an intimate link between the often highly abstract and technical work and that which seems directly related to politics and practical decision making, it is not always easy to tell what the core issues are between Habermas and his detractors and the force of some of the technical pieces may get lost against the background of objections to the work that are more practically orientated. Be that as it may, it is true that Habermas himself has placed a large burden on the more philosophical aspects of his work emphasizing the more technical justificatory program. The thought here is that although history and contemporary study may show that the communication society may well never have existed, and therefore, perhaps, because of the problems with any such society never will, there is an important sense in which this is bypassed by the philosophical program. That program, it could be argued, aims to secure the blueprint as an ideal rather than an actuality. It is designed to show the coherence of the philosophical vision and persuade of its validity as a regulatory ideal. This being so, it is important to look a little more closely at the philosophical justification that Habermas provides. For it is by looking at the underlying philosophy that we will be able to understand why anyone would object to such prima facie sensible ideas and thereby understand more clearly the idea of a rational society that has discourse at its heart.

DISCOURSE AND THE PROBLEM OF MODERNITY

When we consider the question as to the basis on which social change, particularly partisan struggles to effect change, actually do, or could possibly proceed, it is possible to draw a distinction between those who think that the central category here is power—that think this is the fundamental reality that underpins politics—and those who think that ethical concepts such as justice have conceptual priority. From the perspective of the former camp, considerations of justice may be paid lip service while recognizing that this is a necessary, perhaps Machiavellian, charade to maintain power. Or, following Nietzsche, it may be thought that any such ethical concepts are merely a manifestation of a "slave morality" which is that of those too weak to recognize our "will to power" as the basis of all human activity. Habermas quite clearly falls into the second camp, for it is central to his project that although political activity is about power, power is in some sense a phenomenon that is derived from the communicatively agreed on norms that form the ethical basis of political activity. Indeed, we may take this point a bit further and suggest that pursuing the "project of modernity" is precisely the project of showing how just norms are possible and also trying to foster the institutional arrangements to allow them to become actualized. Clearly, any theory that takes strategy and tactics as the basic phenomena of politics presents a challenge to Habermas.

When Lyotard[7] (1997, p. xxiv) wrote that "postmodern" was "incredulity towards metanarratives," he was, quite explicitly, making the point that any blueprint for society, based on a universalist social philosophy, could no longer bear scrutiny and as such placed himself in the "camp" that does challenge the Habermasian project. The enlightenment idea of material, social, and moral prog-

---

[7]To be sure, when Lyotard wrote, "Consensus has become an outdated and suspect value. But justice as a value is neither outdated nor suspect. We must thus arrive at an idea and practice of justice that is not linked to that of consensus" (1997, p. 66), it certainly does not look as is he fits straightforwardly into the dichotomy between justice and power. But, despite this self understanding with its co-option of the concept justice, it is my view that unless we are to slide into a kind of relativism about these matters where justice concerning clashing ideas (language games) really is impotent and therefore reduces to power, we have to see that modernity requires that we fall back on precisely those resources of rationality and discourse with which Habermas deals.

ress, through reason, turns out to be suspect simply because those ideals themselves, that purport to be the vehicles of justice, lack independent "legitimation" and turn out to be just another manifestation of power. Habermas's discourse ethics with its central premise of speech orientated to consensus is precisely another example of a grand narrative offering a set of universal principles by which all action is to be judged. Insofar as this is what Habermas is doing, it represents no less than an act of "terrorism;" an act of forcing the multishaped heterogeneous "language games" that constitute society into the round holes of an arbitrary system. Lyotard does not object to Habermas's project on the grounds that it is, as a heuristic device, unhelpful—nonproductive from a pragmatic point of view—but is rather objecting to the whole philosophical tradition of which Habermas is part. Habermas's crime is not that he has overlooked some technical detail or other, and it is not that he fails to give due consideration to the metatheoretic presuppositions of his project. No, his crime is that he has dared to engage in large-scale normative philosophy at all. Matters are only made worse in the eyes of Lyotard when the normative content of modernity is cashed out in terms of progress, rationality, justice, and universalism. Why? Simply because the normativity inherent in these concepts is itself not something that is subject to scientific ratification; the ideas are inherently philosophical and the philosophies are merely narratives on a grand scale.

Lyotard's (1997) critique finds fault with the very foundations of the Habermasian project, especially as its central concepts universality, rationality, and the associated concept consensus seem to exemplify all that the postmodernist finds objectionable about the legacy of the enlightenment. Universality is suspect insofar as it requires principles to be applicable to everyone in the same manner and thus, apparently, neglects difference and diversity. Rationality is, likewise, suspect in that it is, first, too closely interlinked with the concept of the universal. This has the consequence that whoever gets to define rationality and reason[8] is also in a position to judge those that do not measure up. The thought here is that there is a direct link between universal rationality as it manifests itself throughout history and the Gulag,[9] where dissent and difference are eradicated by sheer force. Second, reason has long

---

[8]The idea that rationality might be subject to definition, competing ones at that, captures, I think, the notion that even this touchstone of the enlightenment may not be neutral, but is itself an effect of the more basic phenomenon of power. This motif crystallizes the philosophical burden placed on Habermas, for without addressing the radical point that reason is always a reflection of the societies that champion it, Habermas has done nothing more than offer a system that cannot but exclude and alienate those who somehow do not "measure up."

[9]This point was originally made by Madan Sarup (1993, p. 92) and is worth quoting in full: Speaking of the "new philosophers," among whom we may include Lyotard, "they contend that there is a direct line between Hegel to the Gulag. The stages are these: first there is Hegel's invention of Absolute Spirit with its teleology of history. Then Marx relocates this teleology within history conceived in materialist terms. Finally the annulment of contradiction at the end of the teleological process becomes (with Stalinism) an abolition of differences through sheer force. Absolute Spirit becomes the knock at the door in the name of history, of the secret police."

since been suspect because of its instrumental nature. Thus, the thought is that we cannot pin our hopes on reason as recent human history is replete with examples of cultures that seem, at least on the face of it, to be rationally advanced, and yet are capable of, and in some cases recruit the resources of reason to further, some quite horrendous plans.[10] How can reason be emancipatory when it "allows" or "participates in" something like this? Reason is just what the powerful want it to be.

Let us then take Lyotard as broadly representative of the current anti-enlightenment intellectual climate and ask whether Habermas's views on the nature and role of discourse in a modern society are really apt targets for this kind of critique? Let us start with the very idea of modernity itself. Habermas quite clearly situates himself within a tradition that encompasses, for the most part, what we might call traditional German philosophy, which means that he is continuing the "conversation"[11] that begins with Kant, through Hegel, Marx, and the Frankfurt School. Because it is Hegel that Habermas regards as the first philosopher of modernity and it is also Hegel that is cited as an example by Lyotard, of the grand narratives of modernity, let us sketch this Hegelian context that Habermas sees himself as operating within.

Hegel inherited from Kant the idea that reason is differentiated (scientific, moral–political, and aesthetic) and the associated view that one of the problems of modernity is that of providing the rational grounds for the norms that govern these domains. For Hegel, however, modernity can no longer rely on criteria from the past to anchor its normative project. It can no longer rely on authority, tradition or, indeed, religion. Modernity is seen as a new historical age that is conscious of the necessity for constant vigilance regarding the supposed break with the past, and of the need to develop criteria to ground the norms governing Kant's differentiated spheres of rationality in ways that are "internal" rather than imposed from out with the culture of modernity. As Habermas himself has put it, "modernity has got to create normativity out of itself" (1987b, p. 7). Reason itself, as manifest in the new sciences and philosophy (and perhaps aesthetic discourse), is to be the final arbiter when knowledge claims are assessed. Indeed, with Hegel, modernity's emphasis on critique is taken to new heights because the very activity of critical philosophy can no longer be taken for granted. Thus the differentiation of reason, the Kantian grid that is the basis of Kant's diagnosis of the problem of modernity, must itself be subject to critique. In other words, philosophy has to become reflexive. Coupled with the question of modernity's awareness of time,[12] we have the prospect that the

---

[10]One of the most obvious examples here is that of the Holocaust. In some ways this is an example of a very rationally advanced culture: materially, socially, and perhaps even aesthetically too. And yet the instrumentality of reason is put at the service of killing in industrial quantities.

[11]By "conversation," I allude to the literary device employed in his *The Philosophical Discourse of Modernity* (Habermas, 1987), where he imagines all the "great" thinkers involved in a discourse regarding the problem of modernity.

[12]That is the emerging consciousness of modernity seeing itself in relation to history as a whole (Habermas, 1987b, pp. 1–22).

Kantian categories are uncritically historically relative to that era in which they were written and do not fully capture the force of a new age creating normativity "out of itself." That is, the radical reflexivity of philosophy seems to undermine the main premise of the modern project: that there is, available to people, absolute, neutral, reason that can yield knowledge and thus further the emancipatory idea of increasing freedom. If reason itself is historically relative—it reflects the society of the day—then the prospect of progress along enlightenment lines is dim. This radical reflexivity actually ushers in the prospect that history will (and must be) just the story of change, not progress.[13] Furthermore, it is precisely this kind of critique that lies behind postmodern approaches.

Hegel's attempt to resolve the problem of modernity with history becoming the story of the universal subject—absolute reason—finally becoming aware of itself is, Habermas agrees (with Lyotard), a failure. Its all-encompassing unity of absolute reason seems to deny any place for the individual and so only represents freedom in a highly contentious and ambiguous way. Absolute reason becomes conscious of itself in the form of a rational state. Freedom is thus the freedom to accept the principles of the rational state, but of course, if the individual is not free in this sense, then he or she must be forced to be free. In other words, there is the very real danger of modernity becoming totalitarianism. Indeed, Habermas is obviously keen to distance himself from this.[14] However, whereas those such as Lyotard would want to see the Hegelian failure as evidence that there is no emancipatory potential inherent in reason, Habermas remains convinced that there is a way out of this philosophical dilemma.[15]

So is this just another metanarrative? Are the instincts of those who reject the aspirations of a project of modernity correct? Perhaps, but it is worth pointing out how Habermas does defend his vision of a discourse society. If we are in a position to understand the general background to the problem of modernity and those that reject any solution along Habermasian lines for reasons that amount to a general suspicion of the whole enlightenment legacy, then we are also now in a position to appreciate what the stakes are, at least through Habermas's eyes. Do we try and

---

[13]This rather abstract point is structurally analogous to debates within the Philosophy of Science that address the implications of Thomas Kuhn's (1970) work. Imre Lakatos's (1970, p. 178) charge that Kuhn reduced the concept of scientific progress to "mob-psychology" carries the implication that science does not "progress rationally" but is subject to major disruptions that have an irrational element akin to faith. Something analogous to this is present in the tension between those that perceive the project of modernity as being about progress based on reason and those who reject this view. One candidate for the latter position is Michel Foucault with his theory of history being the process of dominant discourses being replaced by others, a process that is not progressive but one that reflects asymmetries of power.

[14]It is, of course, not just Hegel that is the problem. If Hegel's attempt to outwit the "dialectic of enlightenment" by conceiving reason as totalizing and embodied in the state leads to totalitarianism, then so too, it may be argued does Marx's materialist version of Hegel which sees reason as embodies in another universal subject—the proletariat.

[15]This is the dilemma of totalizing reason on the one hand or tradition on the other.

rescue the core tenets of the enlightenment—progress through reason—or do we capitulate in the face of power and agonistics? Do we pursue the problem through the search for universalist principles or do we accept that a perspectival, relativistic view of the world and its activities is all we can expect?

AN AVERSION TO THE UNIVERSAL?

We have already seen how the project of modernity in Habermas's hands has two central, interlinked, philosophical pillars supporting the edifice. One of these is the response to Hegel's and Weber's "entrapment" within the paradigm of instrumental reason by identifying another side of reason, the communicative. Communication cannot exist without, at root, a basis in mutual understanding. The other pillar is the universalism that props up Discourse Ethics. Although both ideas have a lot of justificatory work to do, the concept of the universal is the most important. Even if one accepts the general thesis that discourse is or can be emancipatory, there is still the question as to what makes it fair, just, rational, and so forth, and we know that the answer is based on ideals that have universalist credentials. One could, conceivably, imagine a situation where even Habermas's most trenchant critics allowed that open communication is important or even necessary for groups in forming robust identities and formulating their needs and interests, but denying that this openness extends into the arena of politics where power, in the form of the state or other powerful groups, is encountered. That is, one could deny the universalism here while endorsing a watered-down version of the communication society. So it is important, I think, to look at what can be said in support of this pillar.

The concept of universality is, arguably, one of the central components of what one might call a naïve enlightenment fundamentalism. The thought is that progress will consist of universal knowledge: truths about the natural world in the form of the laws of nature, normative principles that hold for everyone in the form of truths about justice and morality more generally. Thus the search for knowledge becomes a search for that which is universally applicable. The truths of science are not, so the thought goes, relative to time and place, to society or culture; they are either true (absolutely) or false. The same goes for principles by which to organize societies, and indeed, individual lives. Of course, such a naïve view has come under attack from a number of sources. There are those that stress the irreducible differences of social lives and those that live them, such that there can be no universal principles—a one size fits all. Indeed, in these postcolonial times, the very idea that there are moral codes that are universally valid is considered absurd. The dominant mode of thought is relativism, with all its attendant problems of incommensurability and its foreclosure of the possibility of critique of the "other."

What may be said, philosophically, in defense of universality? One central point to recognize is the way in which Habermas modifies the concept from its original Kantian formulation. Kant's moral philosophy is notable for the formulation of the "categorical imperative" where we are told the following: "There is, therefore but one categorical imperative, namely this: act only on the maxim whereby thou canst at the same time will that it should become a universal law." Therefore, the demand for universalizable maxims is a demand that the principles we propose to adopt are appropriate for all. Habermas accepts this demand for universalizability as the starting point for any attempt to overcome the problem of modernity. One major criticism of Kant's view is that it is essentially "monological," characterizing moral reasoning as an essentially individual, private matter. The image here is of individual thinkers engaged in their own private thought experiments regarding their actions and the maxims that they might imply. The question is, can they will it to be universally applicable?[16]

The individualistic formulation notwithstanding, the core idea here is that nothing could be a moral principle if it cannot be a principle for all and importantly that this test of fitness for moral duty is developed without reference to any objectivist or subjective conceptions of "the good" and does not lend weight to any particular set of values, beliefs, or desires. It does seem to try and encapsulate the boundaries of morality in a way that respects the demand that modernity develop "normativity out of itself." For Kant it is the structure of reason itself that provides the universalist character of the categorical imperative. That the framework is minimal is the source of its strength and its weakness. It is a weakness, some contend, because of its formalistic nature; it is empty of content and therefore offers no guidance on what people ought to do in specific circumstances. The strength of this lies in the fact that it does not propose to tell us what to do, only that we can test those actions and the principles so implied for moral fitness.

Habermas takes this basic idea—that reason demands universalizability—and makes it "dialogical." That is, it is not sufficient for an individual person to reflect on the issue of whether he or she can accept the norm; rather, all interested parties must discursively test norms. This principle of morality makes its appearance as one of the keystones in Habermas's (1990) Discourse Ethics, where every valid norm must be such that:

(U): All affected can accept the consequences and side effects its general observance can be anticipated to have for the satisfaction of everyone's interests...

Which in turn supports the principle of Discourse Ethics:

(D): Only those norms can claim to be valid that meet (or could meet) with the approval of all affected in their capacity as participants in a practical discourse... (pp. 65–66).

---

[16]One problem, as R. M. Hare famously pointed out, is what to do with the person who is sincere in his or her repugnant views; the case of the sincere Nazi who quite happily subjects his anti-Semitism to the test of universalization and concludes that it is so fit? Such cases do nothing to assuage the worries sketched earlier regarding the inflexibility and potentially freedom-limiting nature of the universal.

Principle D presupposes that we can already justify our choice of norm and principle U is the rule of argumentation that says what it is to provide such a justification. Skeptics may well ask what of the principle U itself? What of this new twist to the tale of modernity that aims to outwit the dialectic that saw the demise of Kant and Hegel? What could justify the principle of universalisability? Indeed, if justification is not forthcoming, or if it is unconvincing, then even on its own terms modernity may be accused of being self-defeating. Certainly, no purely deductive justification seems to be possible for there seems to be no candidate fact from which such a principle would validly follow. However, Habermas does not leave the matter there, for he is acutely aware of the need for justification. The justification that is sketched relies on the concept of a performative contradiction. Such a contradiction occurs when "a constative speech act $k(p)$ rests on non-contingent presuppositions whose propositional content contradicts the asserted proposition p" (Habermas, 1990, p. 80). So when Descartes tries to doubt the fact of his existence, he cannot because the very act of doubting presupposes the existence of the doubter. It is a kind of logical impossibility. Something similar holds, it is argued, for the principle U when faced with the skeptic. So the burden is to show that " … every argumentation, regardless of the context in which it occurs, rests on pragmatic presuppositions from which the propositional content of the principle of universalism (U) can be derived" (Habermas, 1990, p. 82).

The argument is sketched in some detail by Habermas, which need not detain us here, but the gist of the argument is that in trying to mount an argument to refute U, the skeptic must make certain presuppositions.[17] The skeptic must accept the principles (or, because they are offered as examples pending a further examination, something like them), because he or she would be caught in the logical grip of the performative contradiction. The next step in Habermas's justificatory schema is to point out that it follows from the rules of discourse that a contested norm cannot actually meet with the consent of all interested parties unless U holds the following: "Unless all affected can *freely* accept the consequences and the side effects that the *general* observance of a controversial norm can be expected to have for the satisfaction of the interests of *each individual*" (Habermas, 1990, p. 3).

Once U is secured, then the principle D can also be shown to have more justificatory substance then mere preference. So, U is the unavoidable rule of the logic of practical discourses.

How does this serve to rebut the claims of the enlightenment skeptic described earlier? The concept of universality has a central role in the discourse-ethical project that Habermas advances. It features as the basic moral principle: norms must be acceptable to all and applicable to all. This principle is justified to the extent that the skeptic who tries to mount an argument is necessarily caught up in the performative contradiction. The force of such an argument is meant to be that

---

[17]As set down in rules which themselves are suggested as examples of rules for the conduct of all discourse (see Appendix).

once the skeptic realizes the contradiction, he or she will concede that even his or her position presupposes the basic moral principle and thus the foundation of Habermas's system is secured. Of course, the transcendental argument only works if the skeptic is willing to articulate his or her objections in the form of an argument. It has no force in the face of a rejection of rational discourse. The opponent who refuses to enter into debate is not vulnerable to this argument, but it does serve to demonstrate the limits of reasonableness as well as its normative force.

CONCLUDING COMMENTS

Is the project a failure and must we conclude, along with the skeptics discussed in the foregoing pages, that the desire to have a society where discourse and rational debate are central is hopelessly naïve, clinging to some indefensible enlightenment legacy? In short, I think the answer is no. In the previous pages, I have not attempted to defend the thesis that communicative rationality is prior to or more basic than strategic rationality, so I have not attempted to defend Habermas against the skeptic who argues that he has not shown us that all language use is dependent on some moment where the primary aim is of coming to a consensus. Such a thought suggests that we do not always anticipate that such a consensus is possible, and therefore, if sustainable, may weaken the thesis that normative ideals admit of cognitive validation. The skeptic who consistently refuses to admit that ethical concepts such as justice can be rational except in an instrumental way that reflects power asymmetries has not been rebutted, it is true.

However, let us be mindful of what we still have in play here. The moral principle U secures all that is necessary to appreciate the fundamental role that discourse must play in modern societies. That principle is the test for the validity of norms. It stipulates that all must agree. Insofar as it does this, it provides a basic formal, but not entirely empty, criterion of the moral. What it does not do, of course, is at the same time demonstrate that somehow a rational consensus is possible. The principle assumes that this is the case, it being the burden of the arguments that constitute Habermas's universal pragmatics to support this assumption. Without this premise, it is always possible for the skeptic to criticize the position by pointing out that any consensus will always be de facto, because all such phenomena ultimately rest on power. Indeed, this is precisely the kind of view that Lyotard takes of the matter. However, even without a sustained defense of that aspect of Habermas's work here,[18] it is my contention that we need not yield the ground to the skeptic. We need not, therefore, embrace the relativism and the view of politics as essentially agonistic that this would seem to entail.

---

[18]This part of the project has attracted quite a lot of criticism (Culler, 1984; Thompson & Held, 1982; Wood, 1984; for example), but Habermas has defended it strongly and convincingly (see Habermas, 1982, pp. 269–274).

It is all very well to place an emphasis on cultural differences and the supposed divergence between the values that people may hold and which might therefore guide their action. Indeed, it seems unavoidable that one accepts that certain projects or plans for action can seem perfectly rational in light of the aims that the actors have. What one might disagree about, of course, is whether those aims are rational or consistent. But to say that there can be no rational consensus regarding the aims, or *telos* of action, is to overemphasize difference. There may well be plenty of historical examples, or obscure anthropological cases, of cultures manifesting "other" rationalities, but it is not clear that now, in the contemporary global climate, there really are cases of such radical incommensurability.

It may be true that people, groups, or indeed nations, want different often incompatible things, but it is not the case that we have no convergence on the norms of rational argument that may be used to justify claims to those things. Thus, an emphasis on difference and a suspicion of universality comes up against its limit in the discourse on rationality. Therefore, in situations where discourse is the preferred means of addressing common issues, it may well be that there is disagreement as to what is in the common interest, but at least that is something that could be discussed reasonably. So even if one is not convinced that Habermas is able to demonstrate the whole thesis, it is plausible that there will still be sufficient common ground to act as the basis for processes aimed at coming to shared understandings and rational consensus.

If the preceding point addresses the skeptic who rejects the possibility of rational consensus, it does nothing to assuage the worries of that skeptic who rejects the moral principle U: that only those norms that are accepted by all will be valid. Of course, the argument discussed earlier suggested that the force of the performative contradiction that he is caught in silences this kind of skeptic. However, there is another possibility that Habermas raises (1990, p. 99) where the skeptic is not caught up in the aforementioned contradiction simply because he refuses to be drawn into the "game" of providing argument and legitimation for his position. Recall it was the very attempt to deny certain rules of argumentation that led to the skeptic contradicting himself because this act of negation presupposes the very thing supposedly negated:

> The consistent skeptic will deny the transcendental pragmatist of a basis for his argument. He may, for example, take the attitude of an ethnologist vis-à-vis his own culture, shaking his head over philosophical argumentation as though he were witnessing the unintelligible rites of a strange tribe. Nietzsche perfected this way of looking at matters, and Foucault has now rehabilitated it. (Habermas, 1990, p. 99)

As Habermas pointed out, at this point there ceases to be dialogue. One is no longer talking with the skeptic, but rather about him. Thus the process of discourse and rational discussion is circumvented and contradiction avoided by silence. It is therefore acknowledged that a willingness to argue is a sine qua non for the plausibility of the view that morality is a cognitive business. Now although it may seem that the refusal to speak, to enter dialogue, will avoid the contradiction, it may well be that this is a far more difficult stance to maintain than first appears. Although the skeptic may well turn his back on the moral principle by refusing to argue, he certainly cannot turn his back on the wider communicative community of which he is part. Given that this is not possible,[19] short of suicide or severe mental illness, the skeptic must operate within a community that does have argumentation as the basis of reaching understandings and planning for action. There can be no form of sociocultural life that is not geared toward maintaining communicative action through argumentation, even if this is in a very rudimentary and undeveloped form. No matter how good a "dropout" he may become, the skeptic cannot avoid the communicative practices that being a member of a community entails, and these are "at least partly identical with the presuppositions of argumentation as such" (Habermas, 1990, p. 100). In this sense, we can see how fundamental are such presuppositions.

In the foregoing pages, I have been concerned to elaborate Habermas's core idea, that a society that encourages discourse is more likely to serve the interests of its citizens than one that does not. Put like this, the idea is hardly likely to seem contentious or even remarkable. And yet the radical critique of this idea implies that such a view is merely one possible way of organizing the social and intellectual energy of a society and further, that the alternatives are equally valid. The reason for this is that the philosophical basis for the discourse society is thought to be lacking. What I hope to have shown is that this basis is rather more robust than it might first appear.

REFERENCES

Culler, J. (1984). Communicative competence and normative force. *New German Critique, 35,* 133–144.
Foucault, M. (1967). *Madness and civilisation.* London: Tavistock.
Foucault, M. (1977). *Discipline and punish.* London: Penguin.
Gunson, D., & Collins, C. (1997). From the I to the we: Discourse ethics, identity and the pragmatics of partnership in the west of Scotland. *Communication Theory, 7,* 278–300.
Habermas, J. (1979). *Communication and the evolution of society.* Beacon: Boston.
Habermas, J. (1982). A reply to my critics. In J. B. Thompson & D. Held (Eds.), *Habermas: Critical debates* (pp. 269–274). Cambridge, MA: MIT Press.
Habermas, J. (1984). *The theory of communicative action, vol. 1, reason and the rationalisation of society* (T. McCarthy, Trans.). Boston: Beacon Press.
Habermas, J. (1987a). *The theory of communicative action, vol. 2, lifeworld and system: A critique of functionalist reason.* Boston: Beacon Press.
Habermas, J. (1987b). *The philosophical discourse of modernity.* Cambridge, UK: Polity.

---

[19]One is reminded of the old joke where the student remarks that solipsism is such an attractive doctrine that he's surprised there aren't more of them.

Habermas, J. (1989). *The structural transformation of the public sphere: An inquiry into a category of bourgeois society.* Cambridge, UK: Polity.

Habermas, J. (1990). Discourse ethics: Notes on a program of philosophical justification. In X. XXXX (Ed.), *Moral consciousness and communicative action* (pp. 43–116). Cambridge, MA: MIT Press.

Habermas, J. (1996). Modernity: An unfinished project. In M. P. D'Entreves & S. Benhabib (Eds.), Habermas and the unfinished project of modernity (pp. 38–55). Cambridge, UK: Polity.

Kemp, R. (1985). Planning, public hearings and the politics of discourse. In J. Forester (Ed.), *Critical theory and public life* (pp. 177–201). Cambridge, MA: MIT Press.

Kuhn, T. (1970). *The structure of scientific revolutions.* Chicago: University of Chicago Press.

Lakatos, I., & Musgrave, A. (Eds.). (1970). *Criticism and the growth of knowledge.* Cambridge, England: Cambridge University Press.

Lyotard, J-F. (1997). *The postmodern condition: A report on knowledge.* Manchester, UK: Manchester University Press

McCarthy, T. (1985). *The critical theory of Jürgen Habermas.* Cambridge, MA: MIT Press.

Sarup, M. (1993). *Post-structuralism and postmodernism.* Hemel Hempstead, UK: Harvester Wheatsheaf.

Stephens, M. (1994, October 23). Jürgen Habermas: The theologian of talk. *Los Angeles Times Magazine,* p. 26.

Thompson, J. B., & Held, D. (Eds.). (1982). *Habermas: Critical debates.* Cambridge, MA: MIT Press.

Wood A. (1984). Habermas's defence of rationalism. *New German Critique, 35,* 145–165.

APPENDIX

Examples of Rules for the Conduict of All Discourse

At the logico-semantic level
1. No speaker may contradict himself.
2. Every speaker who applies predicate F to a object A must be prepared to apply F to all other objects resembling A in all relevant respects.
3. Different speakers may not use the same expression with different meanings.

These are rules that by themselves are purely logical and have no ethical import whatsoever.

Pragmatic presuppositions in the search for truth
1. Every speaker may assert only what he really believes.
2. A person who disputes a proposition or norm not under discussion must provide a reason for wanting to do so.

The process of communication
1. Every subject with the competence to speak and act is allowed to take part in the discourse.
2. Everyone is allowed to question any assertion whatever.
3. Everyone is allowed to introduce any assertion whatever into the discourse.
4. Everyone is allowed to express his attitudes, desires and needs.
5. No speaker may be prevented by internal or external coercion, from exercising his rights as laid down (above). (Habermas, 1990, p. 9)

For Product Safety Concerns and Information please contact our EU representative GPSR@taylorandfrancis.com
Taylor & Francis Verlag GmbH, Kaufingerstraße 24, 80331 München, Germany

www.ingramcontent.com/pod-product-compliance
Lightning Source LLC
Chambersburg PA
CBHW052133300426
44116CB00010B/1883